# Success Proof

# Success Proof

Jason Hanselman

With Study Guide by Gerry Erffmeyer

endurancepress

Success Proof is available at special quantity discounts for bulk purchase for sales promotions, premiums, fund-raising, and educational needs.
For details write Endurance Press, 577 N Cardigan Ave Star, ID 83669.

Visit Endurance Press' website at www.endurancepress.com

Success Proof

Formerly published as Not a Rock Star Pastor

PUBLISHED BY ENDURANCE PRESS

577 N Cardigan Ave

Star, ID 83669 U.S.A.

All rights reserved. Except for brief excerpts for review purposes,

no part of this book may be

reproduced or used in any form without

prior written permission from the publisher.

Cover Photo

Used by permission Shutterstock

Author Photo credit

Jason Hanselman

ISBN 978-0-9964975-9-6

®2016 Jason Hanselman

Cover Design by Teal Rose Design Studios

Printed in the United States of America

First Edition 2016

*To Beryl "Grammy" Wilson:*

    *For all of the countless hours you spent typing... reading... and retyping my stories when I was a boy... you inspired me to love God and love writing. I miss you dearly. You are the one person I wish could have read my first "real" book.*

# Contents

The Leadership Obsession........................ 13

Greatness at the expense of people.................. 24

The End of a Dream: Betrayal in Ministry............. 33

Boredom is the real cause of burnout in ministry...... 41

Church HR is not working,
    and why no one wants to fix it................54

Food Stamps, Counselors and Airports:
    sometimes you need to hit rock bottom....... 69

Be who you are. Nothing More. Nothing Less......... 82

Mentors Matter.................................. 95

Bored Meetings, Bad Bosses & New Beginings ....... 108

The Impact of Small Churches ..................... 122

Better than a Rock Star........................... 135

# Foreword

You have in your hands an honest look at what many of us have experienced in ministry and the journey we need to go on if we want to actually enjoy life. If you're looking for the next feel good book or how to book this probably isn't the one for you. Instead of a bunch of quick answers, Jason gives an honest perspective from both inside and out by peeling back part of his soul, showing you the truth of how his life and ministry have gone and how he has come to a place that brings a whole lot more joy. Sometimes what you read may cause you to recoil a little bit, seeing someone's wounds often does that to us. But, if you look and listen long enough, something incredible will happen. You will hear and see the kind of healing truth, liberating freedom and lasting hope that you only find when you get to the end of yourself and find something true; something that has been true for a lot longer than you have been around and something so true it could dynamically change you.

I have always known Jason as one of the most honest and authentic (and funny) guys around. He has a way of looking into himself or others and not only seeing the truth, but shining a bright light on it. As you read about how to be success proof what you are going to find is a calling to something greater, something much more attainable and something worth pouring your life out for. You are going to find the ability to stop wishing for stardom and starting living life to the full where you honor the path God laid out specifically for you. Jason does a really good job of taking the big ideas and putting flesh on them, flesh that looks like the struggles and thoughts and emotions a lot of us deal with every day.

If you will take the time to walk beside Jason as he bares his soul, points out the issues and then points you to Jesus you might just find out that you're not alone. You might even figure out how to live a much more enjoyable life and that could bless a whole lot more people than you know. Here's hoping that one man's honesty and vulnerability will lead to the healing of a whole lot more.

*Michael Gray*

Lead Pastor
Sanctuary Christian Fellowship
Denver, Colorado

# CHAPTER ONE | THE LEADERSHIP OBSESSION

## Success

Billy Sunday and I were friends long before our road trip to Texas. We planned our get away to grow closer to God. In fact, we were able to justify the travel expense by naming it a "mission trip". Laboring under the direction of a missionary who worked on the Texas/Mexico border, we evaded interaction with any natives. I admit, it was no spiritual retreat. As I hung drywall in one hundred degree heat for a week, the only praying I managed was to ask God for His mercy by granting me a time warp to go home sooner.

Fast-forward twenty years. I am praying the same prayer. This time my week is occupied in a cubicle staring at a blank computer screen, eight hours a day, day in and day out.

Not many little kids grow up dreaming about living an average life. I certainly wasn't hoping for an endless commute to a tedious job. Answering phone calls and emails from complainers and putting in my hours in as a "desk jockey" was less than I'd hoped for. I started praying for another time warp to go home sooner. I think many people experience the same disappointment.

Billy Sunday... OK, that's not his real name, but he seems a lot like the Billy Sunday I used to read about in books at Bible College. He and I made our way home across the lonely Texas desert when, to my surprise, he turned to me and asked, "Do you believe you were made for something great?"

I was twenty-two years old. To me, a "great" day was finding enough change to buy a 32-ounce soda and a bag of chips. Before I could even say anything he added, "I've known it for a long time." He wasn't referring to me.

At the time, Billy Sunday was one of the most successful people I knew. By the age of thirty he built a solid business, finished college, and was off to do great things. How did he know his life was meant for greatness? How does anyone know? Average folks like me settle for less, because greatness is reserved for people who are... well... great.

## A Bad Definition

Everything about my life up to that point screamed the word average. I lived in a crumbling suburb in a big city. I envied the kids who lived two miles north in the new subdivision with beautiful green grass and basketball courts with actual nets on the rims. The neighbors behind us converted their cramped back yard into a 3 wheeler track where they rode their ATVs for hours in a fifteen by twenty foot dirt circle. No wonder I hate NASCAR.

What is the answer to the question of success? For nearly twenty years I was on a quest to find out. Honestly, my pilgrimage was more like a Monty Python movie than a real quest. My career in ministry was just beginning, and as a pastor, the

# SUCCESS PROOF

Holy Grail of greatness is a thriving church, speaking tours, best-selling books... and of course a *modest* income to go along with it. None of those things ever came true for me.

I was like a lot of other pastors I know. We blame our lack of success on other people and circumstances:

- Some elder or church lady doesn't respect me enough.
- The people are anti-vision.
- I must have some deep hidden sin in my life.
- If I had more money, a bigger building, and a winning smile, it would be easy for me, too!

If your list is like mine, only one conclusion remains. My definition of success isn't even big enough to be considered average. What if all the blue-hairs respected me, or my church was pro-vision, or I was living a perfect life, or was the guy with the killer smile? If all of those things equal success, something is wrong with my definition.

Most of my ideas about success developed from the many ministry conferences I attended around the country. I frequented conferences in search of the magic success bullet instead of enjoying them as a source for learning and relationship building. Rock Star Pastor would take the stage and make everything sound so obviously easy.

"This is exactly what we need to do when we get back home!" I would declare to my buddies during the session. If we could just do that one thing in our ministry, sprinkle a little pixie dust on it and... *poof.* Greatness would soon follow. I would apply what Rock Star Pastor recommended but clearly something was wrong with the pixie dust.

I had the greatness formula figured out this time. Why didn't it work? Someone smart suggested I should read and listen to John Maxwell, the Christian leadership guru. Was it a not-so-subtle hint that I was a poor leader?

Suddenly, success was about leadership and growing your level of influence. Why did I believe, after investing all of that time and energy copying other people's formulas that this new wave of "leadership teaching" was going to be any better? It was obvious, successful pastors are great leaders, right? In reality, it turned out to be more pixie dust.

## The Next Level and Printed Shirts

It was during an exceptional ministry conference that I decided I was finally fed up with the leadership conference phenomenon. The anticipation was thick in the auditorium as one church planting legend after another illuminated the path to greatness through leading a dynamic church plant. Everyone used the word "organic" in reference to taking *their* church to the "next level." Guys in button up shirts with printed designs on one sleeve, skinny jeans and iPhones traveled in packs. Everyone... and I mean everyone... *looked* like leaders. It didn't take long before I realized I didn't belong.

Who doesn't want an organic church, cool clothes and a hip phone? Why would anyone give up on that? I was tired of the proliferation of "quick fix" remedies and copycat curriculum. As the conference came to a close, I came to an uncomfortable realization -- I am never going to be *that* kind of leader.

# SUCCESS PROOF

## Out for a Walk

One of the worst things to realize about leadership is discovering you aren't one. John Maxwell says it like this, "If no one is following you, you're just out for a good walk." The unspoken application I found at leadership conferences was this: BIG followings are the measure of a leader... and nothing else. So, a person has to have a *huge* personality, a *huge* ego (masked as confidence), and/or a *huge* idea to gather a *huge* following. I was not going to pressure myself anymore to secure *that* holy trinity of *huge* leadership traits.

Leadership is good. Leaders help make things happen; John Maxwell is no exception. Here is my issue: I'm disappointed in the way so many church leaders worship leadership. "I love ME some ME" is the silent mantra. Why do so many modern leaders want to build a self-serving Kingdom?

It could be that many of the people who stand on stage at large conferences don't really desire the spotlight. In their defense, many of the great speakers and leaders I've heard will usually encourage a lifestyle of humility and service. The nationally recognized teachers and leaders offer good leadership principles to use, but they don't have *the* script to create a great and successful ministry in every church. The underlying problem in my heart wasn't leadership... it was envy.

## God Doesn't Care

Why would God lead me to a place where I would be *forced* to envy other leaders? Yep, that's messed up, and I knew it. But in my anger at God I took the next leap of logic. If leadership is so important, you would think that God would be a better leader. He should lead me to places of success and greatness. In fact, I remember reading somewhere (probably in a Maxwell book) that good leaders put their followers in positions to succeed. From my perspective, and you won't like this, I started to see God as a terrible leader.

Leadership is a competitive game. A lot of books ask leaders to rank themselves and their team in numeric order. You'll hear them say, "I want to be a level five leader…" Or, "I'm an eight or nine, but my team is a bunch of fours and fives." Of course, most people who perceive themselves as a leader will always rank themselves at the top. So, when I evaluated God's leadership skills, I was only doing what I was taught. Who knows, maybe all of those leadership conferences and books were finally coming in handy.

And then, God got my attention with these words:

*"God doesn't care if you think He is a good leader or not."*

God has a great sense of humor because I heard that phrase at a Christian conference. After five years of successfully avoiding conferences, I reluctantly accepted an invitation to attend a Christian business leader breakfast. The speaker said, "God doesn't care if you think He is a good leader or not." I couldn't believe my ears.

## A History Lesson on Leadership

If God really cared what we thought about His leadership, the Bible would never have gone to print because even His most faithful supporters had trouble following the very Person who created leadership.

# SUCCESS PROOF

*Adam and Eve*

It only takes two chapters before we see an outright rejection of God's leadership. Adam and Eve ignore God and rebel against Him. In fact, they even go so far as to blame God for their mistake. Adam tells God, "The woman whom you gave to be with me, gave me the fruit of the tree, and I ate it (Genesis 2)." Translation? "If you didn't decide to put her in the garden with me, none of this would have ever happened." Does that sound like "level five" leadership to you? No way.

*Abraham*

Even the father of the Hebrew nation, Abraham, had trouble following. Actually, it's more accurate to say he deliberately ignored God's leadership. Genesis 12:10 is a glaring example. It says, *"Now there was a famine in the land. So Abram went down to Egypt to sojourn there, for the famine was severe in the land."* God was leading Abraham anywhere but Egypt at that time. Fast-forward to chapter 16 in Genesis and to see the results. Abraham fathers a child with an EGYPTIAN named Hagar. He navigated around the famine, but he initiated a racial and religious feud that exists today between the descendants of Ishmael and Isaac. Not exactly what Jim Collins describes as "Good to Great."

*Exodus*

Exodus is a case study in failed leadership. Not even Charlton Heston could lead that bunch of stubborn people. Enough said. And yet, we have a detailed account of their whining, wandering and wanton disregard for leadership. How that story made it in "The Book," I'll never know.

# JASON HANSELMAN

*Samuel*

You know your leadership is in trouble when people openly ask for someone else to lead. Even I know that's a bad sign. Think about this statement, "But the thing displeased Samuel when they said, 'Give us a king to judge us.' And Samuel prayed to the Lord. And the Lord said to Samuel, 'Obey the voice of the people in all they say to you, for they have not rejected you, but they have rejected me from being king over them (1 Samuel 8:6-7)." I usually avoid politics, but I think I'm smart enough to vote for God over any other candidate. God accepts the decision of some committee? Maybe not even God can fight city hall.

*The Twelve*

Things don't get any better in the newer parts of the Bible either. Jesus' disciples are constantly looking for ways to inflate His notoriety and popularity. They know who He is, and they are ready for Jesus to exert His leadership. They mount a campaign for Him to take over the world, and everywhere they went they proudly wore their "Vote for Jesus" buttons. Jesus wanted to lead those guys in far greater ways than they could even imagine… and it had little to do with sitting on some gold-plated seat in the middle of a desert. The only people who seem to recognize his leadership are prostitutes, thieves and children. He didn't get much of a hearing with high and powerful religious leaders who were on "the speaking circuit," they made sure to kill his bid for election… literally.

*The Church*

With all of the research on Christian leadership, servant leadership, and church leadership, shouldn't the church be excellent in the execution (maybe that's a poor word choice) of Jesus' leadership? We have the manual. God really asks us to do one thing, "Go and make disciples of all nations…" Why do so many of us reject His leadership in our lives, and His command to go make disciples? Maybe a lot of people are like me – afraid. I'm afraid I won't know enough, or won't be convincing enough, or won't be enough. I'm rejecting God because I'm afraid of rejection.

## Great Purpose

God is not surprised when people reject His leadership, even when those people are giants of the faith. That's not the point. The point is this: God doesn't care if you think He is a great leader. And, we should stop caring how other people perceive our leadership, too. The mark of success is not how many people are following your lead, it's how you steward the responsibilities God has given you.

Yes. I used the word stewardship and your first thought is money and tithing. Relax. Take your hand off your wallet. ***The kind of stewardship I'm describing involves finding your deepest values and sticking to them.*** It means even if you are offered the position with a lot of power and influence, maybe you should turn it down to find work that gives you more flexibility to be home with your kids. Or maybe it does mean you get to step into a position of incredible influence, but you use your leadership to advance God's agenda and not your own.

If anyone would understand the concept of finding and living out their core values, you think it would be pastors. If that were true, I wouldn't be writing this book. The allure of power that comes from leading a large ministry is appealing, and many aspiring pastors sell out their values to get there. I'm not throwing any stones here... I chased after the same dream and discovered it wasn't really what I wanted out of life and ministry. The only thing that got my attention was a dose of reality and the pain that came with it to get my attention. (You can skip to chapter two if you want to read that story now.)

Twenty years of thinking about greatness was almost wasted. Just like all of the heroes of the faith, I thought I had a better idea than God. Not so much. The secret is discovering the values you hold most dearly and acting upon them in a way that is pleasing to God. For me, I think simple and small are the best ways to steward the gifts God has given me. Thankfully, "mega church" leaders like Bill Hybels took the opposite approach to mine so that the rest of us can reap the benefits of his ministry.

Chip and Dan Heath say it best, "Two people making the same decision might make polar opposite choices – and they might both be wise to do so!"[1]

## Final Question

I recently contacted the friend from the Texas road trip and asked him, "Do you remember when you asked me if you were meant for greatness?" Long pause... "Do you think you ever found it?" Most people are annoyed with my weird questions and sense of humor, but not this guy. He gets me. I think. He wanted to know why I was asking.

[1] Heath & Heath. 2013. Decicive: How to Make Better Choices in Life and Work. Crown Publishing

# SUCCESS PROOF

"Well, I'm trying to write the book called: <u>Success Proof</u>, but I feel like Billy Crystal in *Throw Mama From the Train*… you know the part where he can't quite write the first line? That's how I feel right now trying to write about your question about greatness." He interrupted and told me I sounded more like Danny Divito's character – the guy who is a complete hack at writing. "Really?! Just answer the question – did you find greatness or not?"

# CHAPTER TWO | GREATNESS AT THE EXPENSE OF PEOPLE

## It's Not Worth It

Looking back over my journey to find greatness and success had me wondering if I wasn't chasing it like Commodus from the Movie **Gladiator**. One of the most telling scenes from the movie is when he rides a white horse to the German front, but his father won't let him join the troops because the war has already been won. Commodus craves, but never finds, the validation of his father, the Senate, and even his rival, Maximus. He never gets validated because he's more interested in promoting his own greatness -- always at the expense of innocent people. That opening scene with Commodus on a white horse is a metaphor for the rest of the movie... and in many ways, for my quest to find greatness.

## Leader Envy

It was three in the afternoon when I arrived at the coffee shop, and I was thirty minutes early. This was my chance to take my career to the next level, and the guy I was meeting with was going to help me get there. As far as church leadership is concerned, he had the pedigree: mega church pastor, circuit speaker, and leader of leaders... I couldn't believe he agreed to meet with me for the afternoon. Mega Pastor was everything I thought I wanted to be.

# SUCCESS PROOF

I have leader envy issues.

The kid behind the coffee counter was getting annoyed with me for taking so long to place my coffee order, but I had to make the right choice. If I went with my usual non-fat latte, that might scream boring. I know I'm boring, but I didn't want Mega Pastor to know I knew. Or maybe I should go for the mocha? Then again, a mocha might seem too feminine. No way I was going near the smoothies and other froo-froo drinks. "I'll take a tall drip," I said feeling confident a cup of black coffee would appear manly. Maybe I was over thinking this a bit...

I had just enough time to slip my coffee into a hot sleeve, shuffle though some magazines and settle into a corner of the coffee shop before Mega Pastor arrived. My heart was pounding when I noticed him make his way from the front door over to the table. I could have sworn the rows of chairs parted in front of him like the Red Sea did for Moses (did I mention I have leader envy issues?). "Do you want something to drink?" I offered. He declined. "No, I'm not a coffee drinker." Uh oh... probably should have just gone with the water. I nonchalantly slid my manly cup of coffee to the side of the table planning to drink my three-dollar cup of coffee on the way home.

## 30 Minutes

I suddenly had a flashback to our very first "official" meeting three years earlier.

It wasn't the first time we had met. Several years prior, I was hired by a small Bible College. When I took the position I thought I would be investing in the lives of young people to raise them up for leadership positions in churches and missions. I told myself I was a leader who was building other leaders. However, the rest of the world did not perceive this particular college as a leader factory.

I remember how difficult it was then just to get into his office. After several attempts to schedule the initial meeting, his secretary told me, "You can have thirty minutes with him, will that work for you?" Work for me? "Absolutely," I said, astonished. I was amazed anyone could schedule his or her day in 30-minute increments. Then again, he was a high-powered pastor in a huge new building with a large following. On a Tuesday morning I strolled out of my wood-paneled office to take a three-hour drive for a 30-minute meeting in a corner office overlooking a lake reflecting the Rocky Mountains.

I knew right away that things were not going to go well for me. I showed up in a suit and tie. Everyone else in the building was in a polo shirt, khakis and Birkenstocks. "Your two-thirty is here to see you." I only had 30 minutes, so I didn't waste much time with small talk. My pitch was for large churches like his to work with "mobile" colleges like mine, to develop new leaders for the Kingdom. I used power words like partnership, strategic, and impact. When I was done, he made a comment I will never forget, "Jason, I'm not sure we can help, but I'm right behind you -- rooting for you all the way."

My 30 minutes were up, and I left empty handed, unless you consider cheerleading as a suitable parting gift. The message was clear, "You're not good enough to work with me." And, I believed my opportunity to have a seat at the table of greatness was gone...

## SUCCESS PROOF

# Say What?

Here at the coffee shop, I was given a second opportunity to meet with Mega Pastor. I could think of a million reasons why I should have avoided a second meeting. None of those reasons were powerful enough to override my need for validation from Mega Pastor. I channeled my inner Tony Robbins, gave myself a little pep talk, and whispered, "Things are going to be different this time – you'll see!"

Too bad my wish came true.

I was banking on this second meeting to be big. Why? The circumstances were different. This time, Mega Pastor was no longer with his thriving ministry. As for me, I was suffering from fatigue and looking for something new. In some ways, we were in the same place. Even though he was no longer a mega church pastor, I was meeting to ask him to help teach some classes for the college because he still had name recognition. I think I prefaced the invitation to the meeting by asking for his advice on what to do next with our program.

We were way past the 30-minute mark in our conversation when we began to talk about leadership. Even though he had led thousands, he was still eager to lead something significant again. "I'm bored, and my wife tells me the only time I'm happy is when I'm leading a church," he said. In the very next breath Mega Pastor invited me to consider joining his church planting team. He had dreams of creating something fresh and innovative – we would be a Cool Church.

"Say what?" This was a bona fide invitation to grow under a leadership guru and find wild success … and suffering for Jesus, of course.

I drove home savoring my cold cup of coffee believing my search for success had finally come to fruition. A legend in ministry was inviting me to join his team and lead a church. His vision was huge, and included a mega church of thousands one day. I was in all the way. No more small time ministries for me. This was the pot of gold at the end of the rainbow, and I wasn't going to let it vanish.

## Battle Plans

The truth is I was in love with the idea of success. Getting to a place of success is never a linear journey. In other words, the road takes unexpected twists and is difficult along the way. Unless a team of individuals is deeply committed to one another, the casualties of war can be costly, as I would soon learn.

Even though we were dubbing ourselves the Cool Church, we really did a lot of "churchy" things, like having staff meetings. Without a space of our own, we did what a lot of other trendy churches do… we picked a coffee shop for our meetings. As a former college administrator, I was used to meetings, agendas and filling up hours with endless words. Even though we were the new Cool Church in town, all of our meetings strangely resembled the very traditional church meeting – we accomplished very little in our meetings too.

By the third meeting I got a little nervous about the condition of our team. I ordered a plain latte and headed back to our usual meeting spot, thinking I was the first to arrive. I nearly dropped my coffee when I noticed a new dynamic to the team already seated and waiting for me: Mega Pastor,

# SUCCESS PROOF

Junior and Mrs. Mega Pastor were at the table. Our team of three was now four!

The first item on the agenda was to announce our new children's director – Mrs. Mega Pastor. Of course we couldn't pay her a salary, but the decision was finalized… in the Mega home… the night before. The reasoning was simple: someone should represent the voice of the children in staff meetings. We didn't vote on it, but I think I might have lost that one by a narrow three to one count.

And then, the fireworks started. Mega Pastor laid out an idea to mobilize the church and get involved in the community… but Mrs. Mega was not in favor of it. She thought she had a better idea. Back and forth the argument went between Mega and his wife. Family feuds in private places are uncomfortable enough, but those in public are really uncomfortable. Getting in the middle of someone else's public family feud is *awkward*.

It was an epic showdown, and it ended with one statement by Mega Pastor, "Mrs. Mega… *shut up!*"

Um, did he just tell the new "Children's Director" what I think he did? Yes. The two minutes of awkward silence that ensued confirmed I actually heard him tell her to shut up.

It's no wonder we never turned the corner. We did not really ever reach the status of "Cool Church." The dreams of creating something exciting and new dissolved for me almost immediately. Our demise was the result of three underlying factors. A lot of churches suffer from these "success proof" principles:

1. We were running from something, and not to something. Remember, Mega pastor was no longer leading a thriving ministry. From the bits and pieces of his story that he shared, he claimed he was blindsided. Now, he was out to prove he could lead again, and prove his old leadership team wrong. Funny, someone who knew the heights of success still wanted and needed to be validated just as much as I did. Maybe it was the first time he'd heard, "You're not good enough to work with us." The exact words Mega Pastor spoke to me echoed from the past.

2. **Blood is *thicker* than water.** Mega Pastor had serious trust issues with staff members. According to him, most of his trusted friends had turned on him at his previous church. His solution? He hired Mega Pastor Junior (a.k.a. his son) to lead our music. Don't get me wrong, Junior has rock star talent, but family dynamics usually trump business relationships. Most of my friends warned against me about joining a team where I would be the "un-holy" member of the Trinity (you know, Father, Son and me). Add Mrs. Mega to the mix, and I didn't have a fighting chance. When times get hard, and they always do, family will stick together no matter the cost. The Mega Pastor family stuck together.

3. **People are *more* than numbers.** All of our planning focused on "the numbers." Mega Pastor said

# SUCCESS PROOF

we'd probably average 300 people in attendance when the doors opened, and then and then grow to 800 in six months. Seriously, I could hear the crowds chanting in my mind, just like they did for Maximus in the coliseum "Jason... Jason... Jason..." My life would be so different in the new city because I would go to Wal-Mart and the people would recognize me and carry on chanting, "Jason... Jason... Jason..." The size of the church was the most important factor in our planning – that's it. We never talked about the needs of people unless it could help boost attendance... people were objects to gain our validation.

## The Light Show

Eight months later the dream was a reality... well some of it anyway. It wasn't the yellow brick road to success. Mostly, we made it up as we went along. I expected to have a master plan of more than a projection of Sunday morning attendance. We needed market analysis and hardcore strategy to reach a concentrated sector of the market... blah, blah, blah. Our great vision was little more than three guys (plus a score of some pretty great volunteers) hauling church equipment from a storage unit to an elementary school in a U Haul truck. Don't get me wrong, I know all great organizations have to start somewhere, but this was far less of a dream than we discussed.

Our very first Sunday was exciting, counting every head that showed up. Week in and week out we transformed an elementary gym into a rock concert – complete with multi-colored lights, a stage, black curtains and enough electronic cable to make Gene Simmons jealous. Cool Church was born… and we were exactly like everyone else who opted for a modern worship service.

- We were transparent and relevant.
- We had professional musicians.
- We used hip graphics.
- We welcomed everyone.
- We even got tattoos!

It was like we were the "field of dreams" of churches– if you rock out, they will come.

So why did it feel like something was missing?

# Chapter Three | THE END OF A DREAM: BETRAYAL IN MINISTRY

## Prison Ministry

Two and a half years later, our team was still meeting in coffee shops. It was out of necessity, not because it was hip. In other words, we couldn't even afford a wood paneled office. The new church started, but the luster had worn off the electric guitars. We were not leading a church of thousands... it wasn't even a church of two hundred. What happened? We were solidly funded... we had a team of solid leaders... we had a solid launch team... and we had an amazing vision.

It didn't take a Ph. D. in statistical analysis to know we were not on pace to become a mega-church. Ever.

Tuesday afternoon staff meetings with the Mega Pastor crew became especially painful. Every week was a hand wringing session about how to get more people to come and be a part of our Sunday event.

Our meetings were tense because I was learning that "real" leaders never admit fault. It is the job of the leader to assign blame, and in a very small church, only a handful of people get targeted. We had a litany of excuses for why we couldn't make it over and maintain 200 people. Church growth guys understand why 200 is so important to reach before year two… it's one of the best indicators of success and a path to a "big church." Some of the usual excuse suspects were: the weather was bad, it was a holiday, people are on vacation, we need to get the word out, and this is a tough community to reach. My personal favorite was: we haven't gotten through the veneer of people's lives yet. It sounded so spiritual.

One bright, sunny Tuesday in May, I heard the reason for the church's slow start and impending demise. Me. Instead of a roaring crowd cheering my name in victory, I heard jeers. This was my Commodus on a white horse moment… and I felt very foolish.

"This is really hard for me to do," said Mega Pastor, "but we have to lay you off. The money just isn't there to support three staff members." Stunned silence. "It's so hard because I see the faces of your kids and imagine them crying." More silence. "Listen, you're the best leader who has worked for me… and you know if there is anything I can do to help you get work, I will." It was the same thing I heard years before in his corner office when he said, "Jason, I'm not sure we can help, but I'm right behind you -- rooting for you all the way."

Like a noble pastor I said, "Thank you so much for the opportunity brother. It has been an honor to labor alongside you for the Lord. God bless you, friend, for your honest and sincere evaluation."

It was like the dentist telling me the shot he was about to administer would only pinch a "little." It was excruciating. I didn't say much. I gathered my things drained my coffee

# SUCCESS PROOF

cup and left. That was a crushing moment in my quest to be a great and successful leader.

What was I supposed to think? What would you do? I know what I dreamt about doing. I wanted to stand up and pound him in the nose... but I wouldn't last very long in a prison ministry. Truthfully, even though it wounded me deeply, I was better off because of the valuable lessons failure taught me.

## Dark Days of Doubt

How was I going to explain this to my wife and kids? We moved 800 miles across the country to get on the bandwagon, and now we didn't have a seat on the bus. Where would we go? What would we do? Why is this happening to me, God?

My confidence as a leader vanished. I was angry with myself because I saw the signs and knew it was coming, but I denied the reality of the situation. In a lot of ways, I blamed myself for the "failure" of the church and my ministry. Maybe if I had done more, or was more creative, or could influence more people to join our church I would still have a job. None of that was true, but I believed it anyway.

It was difficult to leave my place of doubt and disappointment. When a person falls into depression, it takes the help of others to rise out of the mess. I am grateful for the friends who came to my rescue. They reminded me of a couple of things: (1) failure is not fatal, and (2) you influenced more people than you will ever know by being a genuine friend. The real hero through it all was my amazing, solid, brilliant, loving wife who continued to love and support me – her courage was incredible.

## Leadership 101

Eventually, the pain lessened, and I took some to reflect to better understand how my golden ticket got tarnished. No one ever wants to learn from suffering, but at least I was beginning to understand it was not all in vain. The many conversations I had with my closest friends after my world imploded helped me discover what I am best at and what I needed to leave behind. One of the greatest gifts in the world is to discover the ONE THING that drives you, or the thing that you believe is your main purpose in life. And, success for the sake of success cannot be a thing. Before I could uncover my purpose, I needed to learn a couple of valuable leadership lessons.

### *LEADERSHIP LESSON #1*

"You are what you are becoming."[2]

Only follow people you want to become. The reason is simple; you will always become whom you follow. Spend some serious time evaluating who you want to be, and then choose a ministry that best compliments your deepest values. Find *that* ministry and *those* people, and you will feel good about who you are becoming.

It was a hard lesson for me to learn, but I was really only working to make Mega Pastor's dream come true. Even if the church had grown to thousands… I don't think I would have

---

2   Nancy Leigh DeMoss, Lies Young Women Believe

been happy. Although it was too late, I realized very soon after moving across the country that I did not want to be like Mega Pastor. Once my usefulness was outlived, I was seen as an object taking up valuable resources needed to build his personal empire.

The leadership lesson was coming full circle. Not only does God not care if you think He is a good leader, empire builders don't care either (but for a much different reason). Empire builders only see themselves and the next conquest on the horizon. My ambition was to prove my worth to another person... and it backfired. Mega Pastor was probably trying to catch the eye of other mega leaders. When my time was up trying to impress Mega Pastor, I had one thought, "I don't think I'm ever going to be enough."

Instead, my real aim should have been to be more like Christ. He's a leader worthy of emulation. I've never heard Him tell me, "I don't think you're good enough for me to invest my time in anymore." I don't have to be anyone but myself to draw Jesus' attention, and He is pleased.

## *LEADERSHIP LESSON #2*

This one isn't new, but it is more true to me now than ever before: honesty is ALWAYS the best policy. I'll start with myself. I was not honest. My one desire was to find validation from other church leaders... to see my name in *Christianity Today* or *Church Growth Magazine*... I wanted to be great. Success is fleeting, and for me, chasing after it did damage to my soul.

Be honest with your team, and if you cannot, find a better

team. I was choosing a chance at the limelight (and I will get into this story later). And, I was afraid to have a conversation about the dangers of nepotism. Junior might have been the most talented worship leader in the world, but Mega Pastor was often unwilling to hold him accountable, so trust was never possible.

Because I avoided the truth, all of my fears came true anyway -- I lost my job and my family suffered for it most.

The final days of my employment at Cool Church were hard to stomach. To best explain my lay off, Mega Pastor created a few talking points, blamed his decision on a lack of finances and waited for the situation to blow over. It's no wonder so many pastors leave churches wounded, or leave wounded churches. It was his moment to be honest and help me avoid the very same pain he claimed was the reason for deep depression and suffering. In the end, the empire was more important than people, and it all reeked of hypocrisy.

If this is how you lay a claim to success in ministry, I was done with it.

## Purpose

You won't be shocked to learn that no one called and begged me to lead their mega-ministry. No emails inviting me to preach to the masses. No one even noticed I was out of work for two months. It was time to get over myself and get on with life. That's not entirely true, the people who I impacted the most knew, and they helped me figure out what to do next with my life, and where I could add the most value.

# SUCCESS PROOF

I know my greatest impact is in someone's living room, or over a cup of coffee, or at a sports bar watching a game and having a beer. I was beginning to realize my greatest gift to others and purpose in life is listening to people. Really listening. Simply remembering someone's name or asking them to meet you for coffee (without an agenda) is powerful.

I've helped save marriages, spark new ideas, and build lasting relationships by simply connecting with people. Hardly anybody remembers what I say from a stage in fact, they often attribute things to me I never say… but they rarely forget the time I spent investing in them. Not everyone wants to connect with people on a smaller scale because it never gets publicized – never.

No seminary graduate wants to be the leader of a dying church or ministry. And please, all of you *pious* pastors can put this book down if you're thinking, "Oh my land! How arrogant! I love my little flock of 25 (soon to be 20) just the way they are." Whatever. Leaders who want notoriety for the sake of notoriety, and leaders who think growing churches must be "worldly," are thinking about the same thing – THEMSELVES.

Maybe you will lead thousands, maybe you won't. This book is not going to tell you how to grow your church – you'll need to reference Andy Stanley if you are interested in building a huge ministry. And, this is not a book about criticizing leaders who have large ministries – I'm not sure whom to reference for that. Even if you never make it to rock star pastor status, **you still need be comfortable with finding and living out your purpose, even if it means something that never gets "noticed."** Take it from me, a Christian leader who made huge mistakes chasing after someone else's purpose.

I admit I wanted to lead something great. No way was I content with shepherding around a group of goats (of which I am the chief billy goat). If you have ever tried for huge success and have failed, this book is for you. Not all of us were meant for the bright lights of the big stage. Some of us, like me, were made to connect with a small group of people and make a difference in their lives.

Maybe one of the reasons so many pastors give up on ministry is they are trying to be someone other than the person God gifted them to be – to be the next Francis Chan, or the next Rick Warren, or the next... Maximus. Or maybe, you can stop wishing for stardom and starting living life to the full.

It took me nearly three years just to be able to write those final three paragraphs. Why? I needed to let some of my dreams die. Before I was willing to do that, I was led through some really painful but exciting moments. I will never be who I was, but I have a much better view of myself than the one of Commodus riding a white horse into battle that's already over.

# Chapter Four

## BOREDOM IS THE REAL CAUSE OF BURNOUT IN MINISTRY

My first little talk as a student preacher was delivered in the middle of nowhere, literally. I looked up the population of Farmsworth. It was 450 folks twenty years ago, and today is down to 336 people. This tiny town is not on the way to anywhere. With nine north-south avenues, and five east west, the small stucco church building is easy to find. Even at such a venue, the only way I was invited to speak on a Sunday morning back then was when the "real" pastor was out of town.

The usual crowd of about 25 people assembled for Sunday morning church. It was my first semester in Bible College, and I really didn't know anything about preaching, teaching, or the Bible. As a twenty-year-old kid, I really didn't know anything about life either. What could I possibly say to inspire a bunch of hearty wild-west prairie people who had seen and heard it all before?

What I didn't know was this simple truth: no one was there to listen to me. It dawned on me years later that this dwindling group of folks had been showing up to church for years – usually in spite of the preacher. Everyone has their reasons for going to church, and the rural folks in that tiny little town were far more loyal in their church attendance than I will ever prove to be.

It was 10:30 AM and I was doing my best to look and act the part of a pastor. I shook a lot of hands, distributed a few bulletins, and walked people to their seats. I was awkward, and probably should have been defrocked on the spot. Every pastor I had ever seen wore a suit, so I selected my one and only suit for the day. I looked like a "poor man's" Arsenio Hall in my light blue 1990's double-breasted coat with shoulder pads and loud tie. Not the best choice in a Wrangler, roper crowd.

Even though I was a nervous wreck, I was a happy nervous wreck. Those folks are the kindest church people in the world. In fact, most of the rural church people I know genuinely accept the fact their church is never going to attract a rock star pastor. Rural churches are small, genuine and quirky. This is not the bad kind of quirky where people get into trouble with the law. It's the kind of quirky you experience at a family reunion when crazy Uncle Harry shows up… and we all have a crazy Uncle Harry.

This country church was built eighty years ago and smelled like mildew. Everyone had an assigned pew and dutifully sat in it each week. Even though the musical talent was limited, the church managed to field an organ player who could actually read music. Her skills weren't limited to the keyboard. Every Sunday I marveled how she could play with one hand, AND take communion with the other without spilling a drop.

## Better to Be Short Than Long

The appointed time had arrived for me to step to the front of the auditorium and say something meaningful. It took me all of twelve minutes to get through my material. That's right, twelve minutes to say everything I knew about seven verses in the Bible. It's not a good sign when the preacher finishes and begins to think, "Is that all?" I was tempted to ad-lib, but I didn't. Besides, I'd heard someone say that no preacher ever got fired for preaching a short sermon. And if that was true, I was well on my way to an exceptional career.

To say many of the people were surprised about a short talk would be an understatement. It's the kind of surprise that says, "Really?! Already? Wow! I expected *at least* 30 minutes today. As the flock files out, at least one person will throw in my least favorite *compliment*, "You're going to make a good preacher one day." No one could call what I did *good* necessarily. And, in their defense, no one wants to lie in the presence of God in a church, so it's as close to the truth you can get without outright lying.

## How Did That Happen?

Nothing from my first public preaching experience indicated I had a future in pulpit ministry. Internally, I was passionate about changing lives, but looking out from behind the pulpit, I didn't make much connection. In other words, I was met with a chorus of yawns. How could I be so energized, while everyone else was not? Maybe making real connections in small and rural church world has nothing to do with a public performance. Regardless, some rock star types seem to love the Sunday morning show.

## Adrenaline Junkies

The secret is not profound. Pastors are adrenaline junkies. Rock star pastor or not, most of us think we're the Shaun White of ministry. We need the same kind of rush competitors at the X Games experience when they catch "big air" on the mega ramp. One pastor friend of mine recently told me, "Sometimes, the adrenaline was all that kept me going." Public speaking creates a surge of energy, and once you learn to control stage fright, it triggers some crazy endorphins in your brain. The anticipation of teaching in public starts to really amp up the night before and lasts until after Sunday dinner.

The only problem is the Monday morning crash. It's exhausting to recover from the high of public speaking. Mix in the *helpful* comments thrown your direction after service… many of which are looping in your mind like a broken mp3 player. I've heard it all. "You went too long," or "It wasn't deep enough," or "Andy Stanley was better," or my personal favorite, "Your hair cut looks bad and needs to get fixed." Some comments are genuinely encouraging, but they are not the comments remembered on Monday morning. If you've ever spoken to the "bored again" crowd, you know some of them would even criticize Jesus if He showed up to preach.

One of my obsessions was to search for positive comments on Facebook as early as Sunday afternoon. What were people saying? It was almost better to get a negative comment rather than no comments at all. Negative comments can often actually be positive if they are constructive and lead one to making a change/improvement…or something more. After investing an entire week of your life in a 30-minute talk, you want to know you connected with people. Positive comments sweetened the adrenaline rush, and kept me coming back for more.

## SUCCESS PROOF

# How To Kill an Adrenaline Rush

I remember the Sunday I realized the depth of my adrenaline addiction. Instead of filling in for rural church pastors, I settled into the full-time role of a rural church pastor. Under my expert tutelage, the rural church doubled in size. Attendance grew from 30 to 80. Church growth experts call that a quantum leap in growth – well, the ones I consulted called it that. After some *deep* analysis, I determined my Billy Graham-like teaching was the reason for the growth.

After a year and a half into my first real full-time preaching gig, I really didn't have much more to say, and I was growing restless. What did I expect though? I was a twenty-something who still hadn't experienced much life.

My wife and I loaded our babies into their car seats after church on Sunday and drove the three blocks home. I leaned on the blue suede armrest in our Ford minivan and asked my wife, "So, how did I do today?" I could tell she didn't want to answer, but she knew it was coming because I asked every week – just to fish for compliments.

"Well, you were a little hard to follow," she said, "I didn't get where you were going." She was tired of playing the role of stage critic week after week. After a year and a half, my wife was unable to find the words to help me understand I didn't have to validate myself through public speaking every week. She did the most loving thing possible – she basically said, "You're boring."

My wife is my biggest fan, so it took a lot of guts for her to say that to me. Even though I knew she was right, I tried to defend my points… and nearly preached the sermon to her again. She stopped me. "I heard you the first time, and it still doesn't make sense. Maybe it's just me." It wasn't.

Nothing kills an adrenaline rush like criticism, even honest criticism.

## The Truth About Burnout

Monday was even more difficult that week. Men have such fragile egos, and mine was wounded. Although I didn't think this at the time, I was glad we had that conversation early in my ministry career. Ministry had to be more than performing on a stage, but I wasn't sure what it could be. In fact, I struggled a lot as a pastor in that rural ministry for one key reason – I was bored.

As a leader you attract who you are, and I was the Bishop of the "bored again." No wonder people were yawning through my preaching, they were, for the most part, a reflection of me.

Experts claim burnout is the result of overwork and endless demands on a pastor's schedule. That might be true for some pastors, but my experience (and probably of most other non-rock star types) was the exact opposite. *Most pastors are underworked and begin to drift away from the important to the urgent.* It's hard to preach one more sermon to people who think they've "heard it all", or recruit one more uncommitted volunteer.

Many of the daily tasks seem completely meaningless, and many well- intentioned boards have pastors under their thumbs. After stepping away from the professional ministry scene, I am beginning to understand why pastors believe they aren't seeing any results. They are required to perform demanding tasks for demanding people, but they really are not sure why they are involved with many of those activities. Either they believe they are on the path to a bigger stage, or they are working hard to keep a set of traditions alive. Neither option is very satisfying.

Instead of making progress, a lot of pastors feel like a hamster on a wheel.

For me, I felt powerless. It was obvious I was not going to change the world, build a huge church, or land on the cover of *Church Growth Magazine*. The passive aggressive side of me also wanted to challenge leadership, but not follow through on my grandiose plans. The result was boredom, which may be in the case of a lot of pastors who are not making progress, a major contributor to burnout. Why are so many pastors and Christians bored?

## Something to Endure

Growing up, my family fit the mold for the classic suburban fundamentalist church crowd. We attended Sunday morning and evening services religiously. It was boring. The only real excitement in my church happened when something misfired. Like the time I spilled the little cup of grape juice on my white jeans… that's right, I owned a pair of white jeans. Or the time a non-Christian family visited church and said, "Oh, $#!? !!" during service, in earshot of the pastor's wife who recoiled in disgust.

In all my years of growing up in church, I never recall anyone in our home really being excited to attend on a Sunday morning. Church was something you endured. And no, my parents were not hypocrites – they were just simple people trying to live a normal life and raise their family in church. I don't know, maybe my Mom and Dad actually liked the organ music and the long-winded teaching? We never talked about it, and I was fine with that. I didn't know it then, but I was getting a glimpse into my professional life where I would spend the next 15 years living out a cycle I now describe as 1000 Honeymoons.

## Superman and Kryptonite

Many pastors either leave, or begin to search for a new church within 18 months of their hire date. My theory is that pastors and churches lack purpose, or they have forgotten it. A lot of pastors share my Superman complex. We think we can fly into a church and be so impressive that the church board will bow to our every whim. The kryptonite of church culture is powerful, and it kills a lot of grandiose dreams pastors have of creating mega church ministries. I'm guilty of holding churches in contempt because they did not share my vision, which was really a vision about building my own empire.

Growing your own empire is not an enduring vision. The "count" on Sunday becomes the master of a lot of church leaders. So many pastors allow a number to define their ministry. Make sure your number is bigger this Sunday, or next month, or next year to validate your work. Bean counting is a bad way to live... it's not a very compelling story to tell either, but it's the narrative preachers swap at meetings and conventions.

Many pastors feel trapped especially when there aren't many beans to count. The excitement of the *honeymoon* wears off in a year, the boredom sets in, and the search for a new ministry begins. Six months later, the pastor announces to the church he's had a spiritual experience, and the Lord is calling him to another ministry. Once again, he chooses a ministry that needs to be rescued, and he is just the man for the job. In a lot of those cases, the pastor stays long enough for the honeymoon to wear off, and for the next one to begin. The cycle continues, over and over: 1,000 Honeymoons.

Leaving a church is painful. It means leaving behind people you love and going somewhere else to start all over again. Moving from one church to the next doesn't eliminate problems because all churches have the same problems.

Your church isn't unique. Sound judgmental? Think about it. Your church has power struggles, difficult people, money challenges, growth issues, and members who leave because the pastor did something to upset them. Some pastors and churches handle those issues more effectively because they understand their role and purpose.

## 1500 A Month

It's clear to me what happens when ministries operate without purpose, and it's ugly. George Barna revealed a very dark side of churches when he said that approximately "Fifteen hundred pastors leave the ministry… per month."[3]
Not per year – per month! The underlying cause for the mass exodus from ministry, according to all the research, is burnout. How is that possible? Doesn't burnout happen in dynamic

---
3   The Fuller Institute, George Barna, and Pastoral Care Inc.

organizations, or places where difficult problems need to be solved? Why is it happening so often in slow-moving cathedrals?

Not all churches are like the one I grew up attending. Some of them are vibrant and even exciting. Churches in fast-paced environments would be natural places for burnout, but they do not reflect the majority of churches in America. Most pastors will serve in a church of one hundred people or fewer where high-stress and pressure is the last thing to sabotage their ministry.

*The majority of pastors who leave ministry are leaving small churches not large ones.* My reasoning is simple; "Ninety-five percent of churches in America are under 500 in attendance, and the national average is around 30.[4]" Large church pastors leave ministries too, but there are simply more small church pastors. Why are so many of them bailing?

## Dreamers

Just about every guy I attended Bible College with was certain he would be leading a significant ministry. We had big dreams and ideal aspirations to shake up the church and change the world. The ultimate validation was to get invited to speak at a local church or lead a youth group while you were *still* in Bible College. It was a good feeling to be at the center of attention on the weekend – rock star pastor status was right around the corner.

---

4  Brandon O'Brien, The Strategically Small Church. 2010. Bethany House: Grand Rapids)

# SUCCESS PROOF

My big break came the year after I graduated. The Bible College I graduated from invited me back to preach at the Baccalaureate service. Of course I accepted the invitation to speak, it was my chance to make a big splash.

I had months to prepare, and I spent a lot of time gathering my research, planning my talk, and thinking about doing something impressive. My big idea? An object lesson. Why not? After all, one of my favorite preachers at the time used them in his talks and he would always wow his audiences. Church crowds seem to love object lessons – they're like flannel graph on steroids. Upon reflection, my idea was not very well thought out. It was a formal service: the students were in their caps and gowns, their parents were in formal attire, and I was in a suit carrying my object lesson – a live goldfish in a fish bowl.

Maybe they thought I was going to swallow a live fish on stage. Now that would be an adrenaline rush. Instead, I just made some point about… blah, blah, blah. At the time, I would have said it was edgy and cool. I would have said it was *real ministry*. Who knows what impact it had? I do know it was short lived, and I was never asked to speak at the event again.

Most of the guys I went to college with dropped out of ministry. What happened to all of those dreams of changing the world? I have a suspicion ministry happened. Like a lot of my classmates, we only knew the "adrenaline rush" side of the business. The day to day grind is more than most guys will put up with on a long term basis, especially if they think ministry is all about the adrenaline rush.

## JASON HANSELMAN

# I Didn't Sign Up for This!

Results oriented people like me want the activity of our work to count for *something*. Some people are content to go into an office every day, punch a clock and get paid for the time they spend sitting in a chair. Not me. I wanted to show up on the first day in ministry and see some results. No one else seemed to have the same urgency. It was a bit like the line President Bill Clinton used one time. "Being president is like running a cemetery: you've got a lot of people under you and nobody's listening."

My frustration with the status quo grew with the special nuances that come with pastoring a church. When I became a "man of the cloth" I wasn't prepared for some of the *interesting* tendencies in church leadership. In some ministries, I experienced several all at once: boards mired in conflict, protecting traditions and not people, and even some I won't mention here. Burnout always followed closely behind.

# Making Some Sense of the Madness

Before you close this book and conclude I am the most jaded pastor you've ever met, please wait. I'm asking the same question you are right now, "No one else made you get into the ministry. Why did you do something you knew would blow up in your face?" Great question. The truth is, leading a ministry is hard. Before I dive into some answers, I need one more chapter to discuss another dark spot in ministry. Because up to this point, I was growing more and more cynical about ministry, and I could see only two bad options:

# SUCCESS PROOF

- The path to "greatness" was to be like Mega Pastor at Cool Church.
- Resign to a life of boredom that leads to burnout... or worse, moral failure.

So, maybe those choices are a little too simplistic. But based on my experiences, and the stories of others in ministry, I think many guys feel like those are their only options. No wonder so many pastors leave the ministry every month. The next chapter presents a possible cause for the 1000 Honeymoon cycle. It's not the only reason, but I have a hunch it's a main contributor for a lot of the fallout in churches and pastor's lives.

# Chapter Five | CHURCH HR IS NOT WORKING, AND WHY NO ONE WANTS TO FIX IT

All of the external signs looked good. The church had grown from 180 people to 240. Our growth rate was more than 16%, and newcomers were attending three Sundays in a row. Why was I so miserable? The short answer was simple; I agreed to pastor a church where I did not belong.

I enjoyed teaching and interacting with the people who were coming on Sundays, but the rest of the work was not motivating to me in any way. It was time for me to take a hard look at how I ended up in the cold basement of a church office I hated coming to every day. Most of my troubles began the day I entered the church HR machine.

## Plenty of Blame to Go Around

The hiring process in churches is an abysmal failure. No one wants to claim responsibility for the turnover rate in ministry. Nevertheless blame and finger pointing are rampant. I can't tell you the number of conversations I've had with pastors who are convinced all church boards are evil. Or, the number of discussions with church board members who think pastors are control freaks wanting to "destroy *their* church."

# SUCCESS PROOF

The root of the problem is much deeper than a "leadership" challenge. Something darker lurks below the surface. No one will say this out loud, but he who has the most influence selecting the pastor, has the most control over the church. Selecting a new pastor is crucial for people who desire control. If you really want to simplify things, a lot of the new hires in churches happen for three reasons: (1) Preserving a tradition; (2) Leveraging power and control; (3) Pride.

A lot of churches think they can make everyone happy with the selection of a new pastor. Sorry… it's not possible. Somehow, churches morph into the campaign headquarters of a politician. Everyone needs to have their say, cast a vote, and elect the person who will kiss babies, shake hands, and find compromise among the constituents. The new pastor is expected to keep the hymnal alive, teach engaging messages, and make us feel proud when he is out in the community.

It's pure cowardice on the part of a church leadership team to try and make everyone happy. Why do we keep allowing the cowardly lion into our church leadership teams? The results of pandering to traditions, leveraging power and cultivating pride are obvious: ruined lives and anemic churches.

## Church Hiring in a Nutshell

Again, the result is 1500 pastors leaving the ministry every month. With such a poor track record, you'd think someone would find a better way. As a disclaimer, my perspective is from a nondenominational and autonomous church background. In other words, my church tradition likes to do their own thing… and suffer for it.

In many cases, a church will not try and fill a vacancy immediately. The most widely used word in these cases is "healing." Just ask someone in a decision making role why they are waiting to look for a new pastor. "Well," they will say, trying to look pensive (or is it pious), "We felt *the body needed to heal.*" You can't get healthy by ignoring your problems! In six months, when the zealous committee of volunteers gets tired of doing all of the work, they demand for the search to begin.

Imagine other small businesses conducting their hiring process like this! Someone in the company is let go, and instead of re-hiring for the critical role, they stall. Instead of creating a job profile and legitimate search for a candidate, they go home and ask their wives and distant relatives to "mind the shop" on a volunteer basis. Volunteers are crucial, but does anyone really believe the work is going to get done? To make matters worse, abdicate your authority by creating an ad hoc committee (where "all constituents of the company are fairly represented") to interrogate candidates. The committee's recommendation then serves as the foundation for the next person to fill the role.

Instead of a hiring process, this sounds like what happens when someone is nominated for a post to fill with the US Government. Have you ever really watched when someone is appointed for some commission or high-ranking role with the government? After endless committee hearings and public debates, the person usually gets the job. The price tag for the appointment is intense scrutiny and even public humiliation. It's painful. Listen, if this kind of strategy is an abysmal failure in Congress, why do we keep using it to hire pastors in churches?

No healthy organization would use this process to hire anyone in the "real world."

Am I saying the church owns the responsibility? I wish I could claim innocence in the process, but I can't. Pastors do something equally irresponsible; we participate and cooperate with these shenanigans. Sorry Joe Pastor, you won't be able to use this book as an excuse to hate on your leadership team. If you are at odds with your leadership team right now, you are part of the problem too.

## My Story with Church HR

Barnum and Bailey could not have set up a better circus than the one I was about to enter. My experience with their hiring process resembles hundreds of other church HR debacles across America. First, a vacancy opens in a church. Several reasons usually surface when a pastor leaves "unceremoniously". The most common are moral failure, incompetence, or a church power struggle (or a combination of the three).

Shortly after my rock star dreams met an abrupt end with Mega Pastor, I began the hunt for a new ministry. Unemployment has a way of muting the senses. By that, I mean a jobseeker will ignore obvious warning signs in ministries indicating the position is not a good fit. I struggled for fifteen years to fit in a "normal" church situation, but it was like I had an addiction to apply at those places.

Two months after the layoff at the Cool Church, I was still out of work, so I did the unthinkable... I sent a résumé to the Bell Church, and it reeked of the 1000 Honeymoon Cycle. This wasn't a "spiritual" decision. I was desperate for work, was an experienced pastor, and didn't have to relocate my family - again. Everyone in the world knew it was a bad fit for me. Well, not everyone, the leadership of the church didn't have it figured out. How do I know? They hired me.

"How bad could it be?" I told myself. The longer the process lasted, I started to actually believe, "These guys would be lucky to have me on their team! God knows I can save the day, otherwise, why would He send me to these poor wayward people." I should probably get some professional help.

The conclusion I have long come to is this: you can NOT fight DNA. Don't even try. Churches are the way they are because of years of habits built on thinking patterns. Learn to trust your gut when you see the warning signs. And yes, sometimes the warning signs won't appear until it's too late. In most cases, you will have no trouble spotting them.

Will you have the courage to turn down something immediate to gain a better long-term answer?

## Entering the Madness

My investigation of the Bell Church started two months before I agreed to take the position. All of the rocks I looked under revealed more bad news in this situation. The church website was archaic. My initial inquires with colleagues and people in the area were not positive. When I submitted my résumé, no one contacted me. I even sent my wife on a reconnaissance mission to check out the service and even she, who is way more optimistic than I said, "Well, I think they need a

# SUCCESS PROOF

leader." She also has a gift for understatement.

Again, it amazes me how offbeat God's sense of humor is because even though He revealed so many unhealthy signs about the ministry… I could not find work anywhere else. I begged and pleaded and said things to Him like, "Why do you want me to do this? How on earth will I ever survive *that* kind of church?" Ever notice how very silent God is when you ask Him, "Why?"

All of my research led me to do one thing: call someone at the church and request an interview. That's right, I am a very dim bulb. Apparently my calling is to become one of those monks from the 17$^{th}$ century who beat themselves with whips to learn a higher plane of spirituality. Masochism will not bring you closer to God.

The phone numbers of the church's elder board are printed in their weekly bulletin. So, I picked up my phone and dialed the person at the top of the list and asked him if the church was still hiring, if I could answer any questions, and to request an interview. I kid you not, the Chairman of the Board said, "I have no idea what we're doing about it." Awkward silence. I fumbled for an answer and said, "I… I'm sorry… I don't understand…" Yet another obvious clue stating the obvious: this church is a dysfunctional organization. Apparently I charmed him sufficiently with my stammering because I received a call from someone else on the Bell Church "Search Committee" about a week later to set up an interview.

My first reaction to arriving on the church property was one of genuine surprise and laughter. The church owns a sprawling broken down campus (I would get the story many months later about the purchase) equipped with a giant school bus parked at the back of the lot screaming 1970! As I looked across the property I was amazed at the number of buildings, weeds, and non-working light poles lying on the pavement.

"Who is in charge of this mess?" I half wondered to myself as I walked into the makeshift office for an interview. A circle of 10-15 chairs was set up in the "fireside room" which is really the former living room of the farmhouse on the sprawling property. No one really took charge of the meeting, but every person had ten sheets of stapled papers in their hands. Many of them had their noses buried in the packets of papers and others were making nervous chatter. Eventually, someone said, "Thanks for coming tonight, we're excited about this meeting." Glad somebody was, because I was on edge from the very start.

Eventually, I realized the packets of papers contained the questions *someone* had given them to ask. One person even said, "I don't see why we have these questions… a lot of them don't even pertain!" Probably not something he should have said in front of me or the "committee." That might have been one of the longest hours of my life, answering the most unreasonable questions to a complete group of strangers who, for the most part, had no business in a human resource meeting. You would not believe the crazy scenarios that get dreamt up in these hiring meetings. "Well, pastor, what if the piano spontaneously combusts in the middle of service – what will you do then?" The only reasonable answers to the "piano is on fire" question depend on the kind of church you want to pastor: (A) Use it as a sign to preach, 'Why Music Will Send

# SUCCESS PROOF

You to Hell, or (B) Request an impromptu rendition of 'Great Balls of Fire."

After the crazy questions, the committee wants to ask uncomfortable questions about your family and their spiritual health. Finally, the "weighty" matters of the faith are addressed... my stance on hymnals, how I planned to reach their community, and if I liked spending time in the homes of the elderly.

Remember, we have to have all "kinds" of people in attendance to make sure the constituency is fairly represented. Everyone who has ever applied at a church (especially with a smallish church) has endured a scenario very close to this.

But wait – there's more! If you are lucky to make a few friends and get out of the first round, the Board room meeting comes next. Almost a week later, I was invited back to meet the elders of the church. We met in the same building, only this time, we descended into the basement of the makeshift office. Someone evidently donated a dinette set from the 80's and wood paneling to outfit the board meeting room. This time, Rod Sterling would be smiling and nodding in approval. Not even the Twilight Zone could be creepier.

As with the first round, we hashed out questions about church growth, discipleship, leadership, yada... yada... yada... The meeting wore on and it was clear they were going to hire me because I was breathing and they were desperate for someone to take over after the six-month preacher draught. I am always amazed at the salary numbers and packages thrown around at these kinds of meetings. Why? Because what I wrote down on my notepad wasn't even close to the number they hired me for. Dysfunctional churches are always under the number they allude to (I think that's how they said it) when it's all said and done.

Numbers aside, I knew I was in trouble when the alpha male of the group proclaimed, "Understand, you are probably going to be long gone before any of us in this room will be, so we are the ones really responsible for what goes on around here." Translation: thanks for agreeing to be our underling.

## The Final Harrah!

Two more "group interviews" a trial sermon and a church vote by official church members (four people out of 150 voted no), and the leadership team finally called to offer me the job. "Great news Jason," he exclaimed. "We'd like to call you as our next pastor." My response went something like, "You would? I mean, you would! Can I have a week to mull it over?" They agreed. In truth, I was hoping God would stop the train and let me get off at another stop. Seriously. I was hoping something miraculous would happen in a week and I would have another offer. No such luck.

I was pretty sure God wanted me to do ministry, but just not at that place because the people in charge were not able to do an effective job. I am not saying the leaders of the church are not intelligent people. However, I do believe they lack courage. They needed courage to stand up to one or two people who were holding the entire church hostage. No one had the guts to confront them and make things right. How bad could it be? I think my next story encapsulates the level of dysfunction.

## What Happens in Vegas

Monotonous meetings grow on churches like mold does in dark wet basements. It isn't until you reach the conclusion of one of them that you start to think, "Am I going to spend the rest of my ministry leading these kinds of meetings?" Many organizations believe in holding meetings because they think activity equals productivity. At the very least, they believe meetings will encourage communication. Nothing could be farther from the truth.

Every church has an "untouchable" issue. My gift is to expose them in the most uncomfortable manner possible. In fact, I am so good at it that I am usually requested to move on to another ministry and perform the same damage elsewhere... in the name of Jesus of course. The process is really simple, and it all begins with a question that goes like this, "Tell me why we do *that?*" It's amazing how sensitive people can be, or should I say, how insensitive I can be.

I was three months into my ministry at the Bell Church when I planned to teach through a sermon series I "borrowed" from another church entitled: *What Happens in Vegas.* It was a little bit gimmicky, but I really had no intentions of upsetting anyone. A few of the blue hairs raised their eye brows at the title, so it was a good thing it was early into my ministry and they had a little house money to play with. The real point of the Vegas series was to talk about building faith in difficult times. Seems harmless, right? Yeah, that's what I thought too... never bet against the house.

## You Have a What?

A lot of pastors I know plan their sermons through "divine leading." As a self-proclaimed control freak, that strategy won't work for me. I get a lot of comfort in life knowing how a calendar looks and what I can expect. My Vegas talks were planned out well in advance and I made sure everyone on the Bell Church leadership team had a copy of the sermon schedule by September.

The monthly elders' meeting rolled around and we plodded through the business of the church including the preaching calendar. Although I sent the material out in advance, I'm pretty sure the first time many of them looked at the agenda was during the meeting. No one had any problems with the Sunday sermon schedule I presented. In fact, I think many of them were happy to get something in advance. A lot of church meetings are a reaction to people problems, money crunches or some other mini crisis. This meeting seemed like a success, when in reality, we were unknowingly laying the groundwork for an explosion of Vegas sized proportions in a month and a half.

My little Vegas series was scheduled for the month of December. No one mentioned a sacred event that happened every year during December. You guessed it, the church had a hand bell choir. Wait, you didn't guess hand bells? Me neither. Even though I had grown up in church my whole life, I had no idea churches were still doing hand bell choirs.

# SUCCESS PROOF

Usually, sacred cows in churches moo loud enough to alert you to their presence. A pastor will usually be advised about them in the interview with a leading question. Someone will ask you, "What is your stance on hymnals and organs?" Or, "The last preacher never wore a tie, do you think pastors should dress up for church?" You can either join the herd, or decide to go cow tipping. But what do you do with a sacred cow in stealth mode?

It was November when I heard about the hand bell choir, and I think my response was, "You're joking right? Seriously? You have a *what*?" In November the elders meeting was a little more tense. The agenda had the words "hand bell choir" on it in bold letters. We talked for hours about the bells, if hand bells enhanced the Gospel message that day. No one wanted to make a decisive move. I really didn't blame those elders for agonizing over the decision and what we were going to say to the people who had their hearts set on a hand bell choir performance. At the same time, we had so many meetings like this where we wasted countless hours on people who wanted to hijack church services for their pet projects.

We made a decision to exclude the hand bells from Sunday morning services that December. My rationale was, "My series of 'What Happens in Vegas' doesn't seem to fit very well with a hand bell choir... let's ask them to play on Christmas Eve, or in the afternoon with a concert dedicated to hand bells." We weren't killing the sacred cow, but we weren't letting it loose to graze on Sunday mornings anymore either.

JASON HANSELMAN

# Hells Bells

Word quickly spread about my hatred for bells. I was tempted to make a shirt that read, "Don't hate the player, hate the bell he's playin!" A seemingly innocent meeting turned into a church wide fiasco. One woman spent an entire day attacking me, claiming I had a master strategy to destroy hand bell choirs (cue evil music). She called my secretary and yelled at her for half an hour, and then she found a way to by-pass the phone system to yell at me for an hour on the phone.

Things got real when she crashed through my office door an hour later to make accusations against me in person for another 45 minutes. "As I told you on the phone," I said, we simply don't think the bell music works with a series titled *What Happens in Vegas*." Her response was so outrageous I couldn't help but cringe. She replied, "I'll have to go back and check the tape to see if you really said that or not." Say what!? She actually recorded our conversation. With a straight face I said, "I think that's illegal." I was bluffing, but it worked. She turned as pale as a ghost and stormed out of my office.

I thought, "Did I really just have a forty five minute argument to defend myself against high treason of bell music?" The real injustice was she didn't even attend the church! At least three more meetings were scheduled to talk about the bells, countless emails swirled around cyberspace regarding the incident, and years melted off my life because of it. If I didn't hate bells before, I really do now. Maybe this is what AC/DC envisioned when they wrote Hells Bells.

# SUCCESS PROOF

It took weeks to clean up the shrapnel from the grenade dropped in my office by the bell lady. I started to think, "Ministry is a complete waste of my life." Some things are worth going to the mat over, and this was not one of them. You can never argue someone out of a tradition. So many church people associate a tradition with a person, and to tell them the tradition doesn't matter is like telling them their friend/relative/pastor or whoever initiated the tradition doesn't matter. It's especially hard when that person isn't living.

Some day I'll learn to just smile and nod... some day.

## Time to Move

A year and a half at the Bell Church felt like a decade to me. My final day as an "official" pastor finally arrived. I wish I could say everything worked out for the best right away. Ironically, I went from Bell Church to work for a Christian counseling ministry as their development officer. Although I was broken and working through a mini identity crisis, I couldn't afford their help. I was raising money for other pastors to come and get solid counseling (I might make this the subject of my second book!) but was not able to benefit from the services I really needed.

Sadly, my story in the church HR maze is not unique. The church has a system designed to place people in positions where they are likely to be unhappy, but feel powerless to do much about it. Consider this startling statistic and solution reported by Simon Sinek:

> Only 20 percent of Americans love their jobs...
> We need to build more organizations that prioritize the care of human beings. As leaders, it is our sole

responsibility to protect our people and, in turn, our people will protect each other and advance the organization together. As employees or members of the group, we need the courage to take care of each other when our leaders don't. And in so doing, we become the leaders we wish we had.[5]

If I could solve the church HR monster, so many lives would be changed... and it lies at the root of the cause for the 1000 Honeymoon Cycle. My book is not about changing the system – I tried to for twenty years with no success. Instead, my story is one of hope and redemption. Second chances are beautiful. In the process of writing my story, I was able to look back and appreciate the sum total of the journey up to this point. Much of my time in pastoral ministry was painful, but the lessons I learned give me hope to try something new. "Recovering pastors" must take comfort knowing they're not alone. The future held the moments of light I found along the way.

---

5      Sinek. Leaders Eat Last: Why Some Teams Pull Together And Others Don't. 2014 Penguin Group: New York.

# Chapter Six

## FOOD STAMPS, COUNSELORS AND AIRPORTS: SOMETIMES YOU NEED TO HIT ROCK BOTTOM

My wife and I walked into a drab concrete government building not really sure of what to expect. I took my wife's hand, we walked to the counter, took a number, and scanned the large open room for somewhere to sit.

Rows of hard plastic chairs hid the padded chairs in the far corner of the room. They would be the only comfort afforded us. After years of preaching against the trap of judgmental thinking, I discovered how very judgmental I really was. As I looked from face to face it was obvious why *those* people were here for a "handout". I clearly did not belong. I'm not even a *Democrat!* Relax Democrats; I counted on your policies to help my kids eat.

It wasn't fair. Didn't God remember we were on His team, and that we'd been generous to others who needed help? Was there nowhere else to turn?

We didn't know anyone in the room and thought every eye looking our direction was filled with contempt. Suddenly, I knew why so many men in these situations hide in the car while their wife goes in to fill out the paperwork. Every fiber of your manhood is filled with shame. Our number was called. The walk across the room to the case worker's office felt like miles of stone I laid, each weary step burdened by my inability to provide for my family.

We took our seat in the welfare office and waited. In that moment, walking away from ministry may not have felt like the right thing to do, but at least I wasn't asking my family to make another move to advance my career. This time, our decision was about putting our family ahead of a career in ministry.

Don't listen to the people who tell you following God **always** brings health, wealth and blessing. We needed a clean slate and a fresh start. The idea of starting over seemed profound – even noble. But, unemployment isn't noble. Facing hard times and trying to feed your children is a feeling of desperation I never want to feel again. I empathize with anyone facing it. Pain is a tool useful to instigate introspection. I needed to take a very hard look at my choices and the reality of my situation.

As difficult as the situation seemed, I knew we'd made the right choice. We never gave up on hope that God was still in control. In fact, we knew the difficult times were still ahead, but the will to move forward was stronger than ever. This, in spite of all the evidence to the contrary, is right where God wanted us to be.

## People, Prayer and Pills

Falling into poverty and entering the "welfare system" didn't happen immediately. Honeymoon followed honeymoon, each position I was offered took me farther and farther from stardom, farther from happiness, and farther from financial stability.

# SUCCESS PROOF

My family progressed from safe suburban education to schools where drug-sniffing dogs attended school more than some of the students. We digressed from inviting friends over on a weekly basis to spending most of our time in isolation. We... no, I made a huge mistake chasing a career. I asked my wife to forgive me and to help me refocus our lives. We sold many of our belongings (including my prized possession of a motorcycle), quit our jobs returned to the place we loved the most to keep our family intact.

On paper, the timeline is only a couple of paragraphs long. You can learn a lot about yourself and life in a couple of paragraph's worth of time. I earned a graduate degree in life. It's easy to look back and see how everything worked out, but the pain and the process helped me recalibrate my life. In fact, my experiences were the means by which my stubborn heart finally heard some much needed truth.

One of my favorite pastors uses a phrase I have passed along many times, "God saves us through people, prayers and pills.[6]" His statement is even funnier when you know he teaches in Boulder County, Colorado. In context, he was saying: get in a good church, pray a lot, and seek psychiatric help if you really need it. A lot of pastors would never suggest seeking a counselor. But I believe seeking mental help is crucial when you "lose your way." Seeking help from a mental health professional is not sign of weakness or a denial of God's power. The opposite is true.

---

6    Burgen. No More Dragons: Get Free from Broken Dreams, Lost Hope, Bad Religion, and Other Monsters. 2014. Nelson Books, Nashville)

JASON HANSELMAN

# A Good Laugh

My first visit to a counselor was really unplanned. In the months following my exit from ministry, I did what a lot of really spiritual people do... I wallowed in my misery. Almost every conversation I had became an excuse to bring up the past and justify my hurts in ministry. Without even realizing it, I became more than cynical... my inner life was toxic. The truth is, I was really begging for help, but always stopped short of asking for it because I had the *right* to feel bitter about the way I was treated.

This is the part of my story where God is going to have a good laugh with me some day. My theology tells me God doesn't laugh at our expense, but I think I had it coming. Seriously, God was kind of mocking me, and I walked right into it.

For months, after leaving full time ministry, I avoided people from my ministry days. So many well-intentioned Christians want to give you their best bumper sticker theology when they perceive you need to be "fixed." They will say things like: "Just let go and let God..." or, "Don't worry, God has a plan for you..." or (my personal favorite), "God helps those who help themselves." If you are the kind of person who thinks those phrases are going to create a "Hallmark Moment"... just stop. Save the cheese for FaceBook.

Facing people from your former life is hard, especially if you haven't come to terms with your new life. I decided to try and reconnect with a guy who is the most genuine pastor I know. He's not like the typical Khaki and polo pastor most of us have come to expect and love. He's a mountain biking,

# SUCCESS PROOF

cigar smoking, straight talking kind of a guy. He's a modern day John the Baptizer.

Mike the Mountain Biker Pastor (MMBP) is quite possibly the most spiritually healthy leader I know. More than anything, MMBP knows how to diagnose and reframe problems. His specialty was solving problems at a University of more than 12,000 students until he took a lead pastor job in a local church. The church he pastors has accomplished much more than singing songs and building stained glass cathedrals. MMBP has worked with city officials, elementary school administrators and community leaders to build soccer fields and restore hope in his community.

He's one of the healthiest and most well-adjusted individuals I know... and he still agreed to meet! At eight in the morning, I hustled out of the cold and into the warm breakfast diner. There he was, in his plaid over shirt, cargo pants and hiking boots. At 50 plus years old, he looked the part of the rugged mountain man preacher. "Dude!" he exclaimed. "Never thought I'd see you back here Hanselman... you must have a good story." We ordered breakfast and he started talking about his latest issue with a person on his board. MMBP is a classic preacher and loves exaggerating his stories. "And then," as MMBP paused for dramatic effect, "I was inches away at the board meeting from pile driving that board member into the board room table!" What a great ending to an anger management story!

"Well... what do you think I should do with the guy I want to pile drive Hanselman?" he demanded.

If anyone was UNable to give advice about how to seek help, it was definitely me. Some people have a way of looking through your soul. I was uncomfortable making eye contact because his sharp blue eyes seemed to be looking right through me. After stammering and stalling I leaned forward, over a gigantic pancake and steaming cup of coffee and said, "Well, I don't think going MMA (Mixed Martial Arts) on your board member is a good idea... have you considered professional help?" To this day, I don't know if he was setting me up, or really looking for my advice (never mind, I know he was messing with me!). "Maybe I should go see my Counselor-Guy... and by the way, he's really well connected and could help you find more contacts too... I'll shoot you his contact info today."

"Where's the bombshell?" you ask – I received two in that moment. MMB should have jumped over the table, slapped me across the face and shouted, "You idiot! *You're the one who needs counseling!*" He could have. But he knew I would have just dismissed his crazy outburst, and felt even more like a phony victim. MMBP actually set me up for a hard fall.

He introduced me to the person who would completely shift my attitude. I was going to look at life through a much healthier lens. MMBP set me up with an absolute jerk of a counselor, and it was exactly the kind of person I needed to meet. Did God arrange that meeting in the diner – did the Mountain Biker intentionally steer me to counseling? It doesn't matter. Only God knows... and I really believe He's laughing... at me... mostly.

So, yes, people, prayer and pills are the means by which God will save you.

## SUCCESS PROOF

# Counselors are Jerks!

The first time I met Counselor Guy was in a well-lighted hip restaurant in a suburb of Denver. We grabbed a booth by a window, ordered lunch, poured coffee and commenced with small talk and introductions. Without even realizing it, I'd let the counselor ask ALL the questions. He was good. He's a fifty-something guy with white hair, deep blue eyes and a round body shape. Everything about him screams – TRUST ME. Couple all of that with a good ole' boy southern accent, and you have enough charm to win an election.

Without really realizing it, I was pouring out my sob story... again. Finally, I stopped myself and feeling embarrassed said, "I'm so sorry, this wasn't supposed to be a counseling session." He just smiled and said, "It sounds like you have a lot of pain, and I am so sorry." Wait. Where's the Hallmark Christian moment? What do you do when someone offers real grace? I mumbled, "Thanks... I appreciate that." He continued, "Why don't you schedule a time with my assistant and we can help you unpack your thinking a little." I was thinking, "What?! No way in he*# do I need help!" What came out of my mouth was, "I think that would be a good idea."

The first session was uneventful. I shared my story, he took notes and asked some more questions. Our time ended and he gave me a bill. Even though I believe in counseling, I wasn't exactly making Joel Osteen type of money. I handed over my Visa and thought, "The next session better have some answers."

Be careful what you wish for.

The following week I showed up early to the appointment. As usual, I grumbled about the parking. Even finding a parking spot is unmanageable for toxic people. Finally, I made my way into the office and was struck by the stillness. The quiet in the room almost swallowed me up. As I slid into the faux leather chair the air from it exhaled announcing my presence in the office. The stillness was so uncomfortable - I almost felt like it was encouraging me to run away. I started to think, "We can't afford this... maybe I'm beyond repair... does he *really* know what he's doing?" Before I could make an exit, Counselor Guy appeared with his clipboard of notes from the last session. "Ready?" he inquired.

Midway through the session it happened. All of that southern charm and hospitality turned on me. "You have some growing up to do Jason..." he pronounced. Before I could object, he went on with this, "Just hold on... not in *every* area, but in ONE glaring place." Reluctantly I said, "OK, I'll bite, go on..." He drew this diagram and explained his statement (hope you like my handmade rendition!).

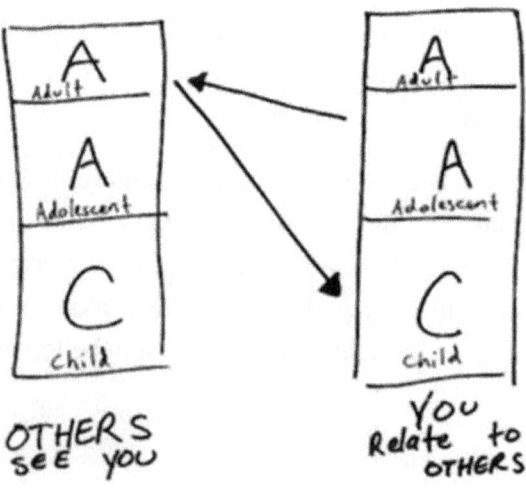

## SUCCESS PROOF

"Every adult is capable of filling one of three roles in their interactions with others. You can be an adult, an adolescent, or a child. You can decide which one you want to be. However, you cannot control how others view you. In fact, many people can only see others as children. Consequently, they view themselves as a father figure in the worst sense possible. No one can ever measure up to their impossible standards, so they prevent others from reaching their potential. Get away from those types fast! Of course, you can perpetuate the cycle by acting like a child by throwing temper tantrums, feigning helplessness. Those behaviors encourage others to see you as a child."

"Sounds right so far," I said practically giving him permission to lower the boom. He did. Counselor Guy continued, and delivered my "ah-ha" moment. The weight of what he said next was like someone peeling off an old scab. It hurt, and it revealed something profound beneath the surface.

"I don't know if you know how others really perceive you," he suggested.

He drew a line from the "Adult" box on the OTHERS side of the diagram to the "Child" box on the YOU side of the diagram, and said, "The adults, or colleagues in your life, view you like a child." I think I said something like, "Well, that's not good news." He dug in a little more. He drew an arrow from the "Adolescent" box on the YOU side to the "Adult" box on the OTHERS side, and paused before adding his next comment.

"From what you told me, and from our brief interactions, I hear a lot of sarcasm in your voice." I nodded, and he moved forward, "That's really the characteristic of an adolescent, and not very good for adult interactions… and if you want others, like the people you work for, to see you any differently, you need to remove it from your speech." Translation: grow up. Most adolescents who feel wronged cannot see how their own actions are stunting their growth. Straight truth hurts… and eventually heals.

Our session came to an end. He swiped my credit card. The bill was just as high, but this time I was not wishing for any more answers. I grabbed my coat and headed for the door more determined than ever… to prove him wrong!

As soon as I got out the door, I unleashed my iPhone to make three calls to some close friends. Each conversation lasted about 20 minutes. I asked my three friends one question. "Do you think my approach with people is too sarcastic and adolescent?" All of my friends paused long enough before answering for me to know what they were thinking. They agreed with Counselor Guy. "What a jerk Counselor Guy is," I muttered. Oops! More adolescence.

Suddenly, so many things were very clear to me. My way of dealing with what I thought were the unfair actions of others was to essentially "roll my eyes." Counselor Guy never said the people I worked with, or the churches I pastored were right in their dealings with me. You can't help what other people do to you. I was responding poorly… and didn't even fully realize it. My warped perception of reality told me my humor was helpful. Counselor Guy told me the exact opposite. My approach was sharp and cynical. As long as I played the role of the adolescent, I would not be able to deal with bad bosses, ugly situations and the challenges of ministry.

Now what? Did God arrange for my counseling sessions? Maybe. I knew it was exactly what I needed to hear. If MMBP had not steered me to Counselor Guy, I can't imagine the bitterness I'd still be carrying.

## Putting Some of the Pieces in Perspective

Taking a few steps back and assessing the damage, I knew I was not the ministry version of Adam Sandler. A lot of my relationships are intact and healthy. In the ones where I feel powerless to change circumstances, or when I feel undervalued, I'm pretty good at playing the sharp-witted fool. Instead of beating myself up over my inadequacies, I made a conscious decision to move. Time to grow up. It wasn't an easy decision to make because one of the outcomes was bearing the shame of unemployment and accepting food stamps. Grown-ups make hard choices.

No more adolescence. No more running from problems. No more blaming others for my situation.

## 2 Year Hiatus And An Airport

The process of unpacking baggage was more than a two-year process. This book is a direct result of my experiences and attempt to recalibrate my life. I almost decided to give up expressing myself through writing. It was simply too honest, too painful.

The eye opening conversation with the counselor was only the beginning of the process. If you are waiting for the "happily ever after" narrative, get a copy of *Frozen*. Diagnosing a problem is the easy part, having the courage to work out a solution is very difficult. In the two-year hiatus I took from writing, things seemed to get worse. Why? My résumé makes it difficult for me to find work *outside* a church. In the end, one of the only companies to hire me was the United States Department of Homeland (DOH) Security. Impressed? Don't be. I accepted a position at the airport working as a Transportation Security Officer (TSO).

It was a great reality check for me. In fact, I had an epiphany while working one long nine-hour shift one Sunday. All of the abuse and mistreatment ministry types (like me) whine about, these people take on a daily basis… and some of them had been working with the DOH for a decade. Think about it. They do a thankless job, for a meager wage in an energy-sapping environment. Day after day, standing in the same spot, looking at people's suitcases full of undergarments and deodorant trying to find some greater meaning in it all.

It was safe to say I was at the bottom of the career ladder – and right where I needed to be in that moment.

Working at the airport helped me re-establish my love for people. How is that possible? This will ruffle a few feathers, but I find people who are not associated with a church to be more honest. Not honest in the sense of truth telling, but in the sense of being genuine about their doubts and questions. Spending time around people who do not profess Christianity was a breath of fresh air for me. And no, I'm not suggesting I think the Gospel is in any way inferior to any other belief system. Instead of trying to convince everyone to think just like me, I want to offer grace AND truth… not just truth.

# SUCCESS PROOF

Once my coworkers discovered my former life in ministry, my days became way more interesting. They had all sorts of philosophical questions about life and spirituality for this "recovering" pastor. I loved it. Some of my fellow TSO mates nearly dared me to defend my beliefs about the exclusive nature of Christianity. This was as close as any of them were ever going to get to a pastor, so they made it known how they really felt about *my kind*.

I have no idea how much influence I had on anyone's life in the bowels of the airport. However, I did officiate a wedding for two TSA officers. They asked for me to preside, so I shared the best definition of love I know – the Gospel. My time was not wasted at the airport. If anything, it motivated me to ask God for a second chance. I needed a second chance to work with people in a place where I could influence their spiritual direction.

Where would I go? How could I convince anyone to believe in me again? I'd been through at least three short-term ministries. You won't believe where I discovered the answers to my questions.

# Chapter Seven

## BE WHO YOU ARE. NOTHING MORE. NOTHING LESS.

### "Pastor Speak"

This chapter scares me. Seriously, I sat down to write it and thought, "How did I get here?" If I follow through with it, I might end up betraying the very soul of this book. I'm tempted to conclude with the best motivation speech line ever, "Vote for me and all of your dreams will come true." It worked for Pedro.

Twenty years ago, I was really (as we say in the Christian culture) "on fire" for God. A lot of my friends and former mentors were shocked when I decided to quit art school in the middle of a thriving metropolitan city and move to a dusty little cow town in Nebraska to study to be a pastor. I was scared to death, but never felt more alive. Finally, my life had direction and purpose.

The only problem is, I have a rebellious side (actually, my close friends call it passive aggressive behavior, but whatever). I showed up on campus in baggy jeans, an earring and a desire to do things a new way. Conservative Bible Colleges and city kids with earrings aren't usually a good mix. Somehow, I found a way to fit. Mostly because I was fortunate to bond with a group of friends who were just as committed, and as unsatisfied with the status quo as I was.

# SUCCESS PROOF

Our rebellion wasn't fueled by anger. It was subtle. Deep down, we thought we were smarter than the rest of the world. A lot of the people I was in school with were brilliant. In fact, one of my best friends scored a perfect score on the ACT. We were going to revolutionize church culture. I think we were not willing to become *just like* the people who came before us. When I look back I realize I had the opinion of an over-confident 19 year old, but we had so much fun pushing boundaries. We had the kind of rebellion that wanted to see things change and get better – not the kind that leads to anarchy.

As students in Bible College, most of us were leading youth ministries and attending youth rallies. If we could influence anyone to change, we thought it would be the broods of kids we were working with on the weekends. Youth rallies were the method of choice for churches in those days to attract hundreds of middle and high school students. Youth pastors were like Moses leading our youth groups to rallies in search of the Holy Grail (I know, I mixed my metaphors, but go with me here)…

For youth pastors, the Holy Grail was to have fun, get kids excited about their faith and maybe find God somewhere in the middle of it. The teens' perspective was a little different. Their Holy Grail was found in pizza and Mountain Dew consumption. The truly blessed found the love of their life.

My favorite youth rally buddy in college was Sam Burro. At six foot five and close to three hundred pounds, Sam was a big bundle of fun and energy. His personality and love of laughter was infectious. We invented ways to have fun when the caffeine wore thin. As aspiring youth pastors, we thought it was our calling to liven up the party. Most of our antics received the disapproving glances of the veteran pastors who came to the rally. No amount of Mountain Dew or spiritual fervor excited the guys who had been doing rallies for more than a decade. To keep us in line, some of them would "pastor speak" us into better behavior.

"Pastor speak" is a unique cultural part of the Christian community. You can make almost anything sound more spiritual with "pastor speak." Just add more syllables to every word and draw out sentences in breathy whispering tones. Words like Gawwwd (God) ... or Looorduh (Lord) punctuate every sentence. "Pastor speak" is supposed to magically make those words mean more, or create some kind of magical effect on the listener as they are whispered into the microphone. Nowhere else in our daily interactions do we speak this way. Nowhere. Maybe the hope is to sound more spiritual. Or, we just don't have anything to say.

Those who are especially gifted in "pastor speak" are able to use it as a weapon to shame someone else. Somewhere between day one and two of the rally, Sam and I knew the musician and his band were in trouble on stage. Instead of encouraging our students to help him out, I challenged Sam to a race. The object of the race was to start at the back of the auditorium and crawl under the pews without getting noticed. First one to the front was the winner.

We got half way to the front, and the guy struggling on the stage stopped hushed his musicians while he kept playing the keyboard. In his best "pastor speak" he said something like, "You guys (insert whispered and breathy tone here), the Looorduh weeeeps when He sees we are not really worshipping Him. He's disappointed when you don't give your heart

## SUCCESS PROOF

to Him (long sigh and deep breath)… I hope if you, or someone near you is goofing off, you will pause and ask them to get right with Gawwwd."

Some kid in the fifth row looked down at us and shook his head. Sam and I rolled to the aisle and snuck to the back. "Pastor speak" guy wasn't amused, but I happened to think Jesus might have found it a little funny.

Christian books are full of "pastor speak." A lot of authors use catch phrases to provide blanket answers to all kinds of difficult questions. Verse like "I can do all things, through Him who strengthens me;" or, "He works together all things for your good" are ripped out of context and turned into self-help mumbo jumbo. Instead of those verses meaning something very specific, we have robbed them of their power. "Pastor speak" renders words useless. It makes people tone deaf. How? It makes a very powerful God look silly as we offer trite solutions to big problems like cancer, untimely death, and babies diagnosed with terminal illness.

This book is not meant to give any answers. I have questions. So, be wary of the author who has a solution to solve your very difficult problem in 10 chapters or less. Either your problem isn't very complex, or someone is using "pastor speak" on you. The trick is to learn to discern "pastor speak" from something truly helpful and honest.

As a person who trusts the message of Christ and Christianity, I don't think everything in life happens for a neat and tidy reason. Conversely, nothing is beyond redemption. The tension between easy answers and living in a mess is the space we have to be comfortable in. Forrest Gump is wrong – life is not like a box of chocolates. Life is more like a cup of coffee – it's often bitter. You can actually learn to love the acrid character in a cup of coffee. It takes time and discernment to know a good cup of joe from a bad one.

I said all of that to set up this one line: The coffee I was drinking... the book I was writing... was too bitter even for my own taste.

After two years of trying to finish this book, I had just about given up writing it. I was tired of nursing old wounds from the past. It would be so easy to "pastor speak" my way through the rest of this thing. My old sermon files are stuffed with platitudes and Christian clichés. I wanted to do what the rock stars pastors do – convert (pun intended) an old sermon series into a couple of book chapters.

I was stuck half between something too bitter, and the potential of cranking out more "pastor speak."

## A Tale of Two Jims: Jim the Rock Star

I love a good paradox, especially when it seems like God is the author:

> par·a·dox' /perə͵däks/
> noun: **paradox**; plural noun: **paradoxes**
> 1. a statement or proposition that, despite sound (or apparently sound) reasoning from acceptable premises, leads to a conclusion that seems senseless, logically unacceptable, or self-contradictory
> 2. a potentially serious conflict between quantum mechanics and the general theory of relativity known as the information paradox

# SUCCESS PROOF

3. a seemingly absurd or self-contradictory statement or proposition that when investigated or explained may prove to be well founded or true

When we decided to step away from pastoral ministry, I had a dilemma. Where in the world was I going to attend church? Simply attending a church is hard to do when you've been "the man" for so long. After studying ministry and church culture for so long, I'm a self-proclaimed church connoisseur. When I walk into a church building, I have some high expectations and a pretty good "BS Radar" system built in. You can get pretty good at determining if a church is for the people, or if the church thinks the people are there for them.

I remember the weekend I walked into a church without the title pastor. No one recognized me as the pastor; maybe my pastoral glow had worn off. The minute I walked in I knew I was in a good place. This might sound a little strange, but I knew it was a church for men. Most churches in America cater to women. Look around your church this Sunday and see how many floral prints, pastel colors and "pretty" decorations are on the walls. If you count more than three places with those things… you are in a church for ladies.

After nearly bumping into several large muscular guys in the crowded lobby I was so shocked that I said, "This is a church for guys." Of course the halls were packed with women and children too, but their husbands and boyfriends were bringing them to church… not the other way around. For the first time in my life, I actually had to wait in line to use the men's restroom. For men, that only happens at professional ball games.

Even after waiting in line at the bathroom, I still had about ten minutes to spare. It was enough time to grab some coffee before finding a seat. Just like every other church, this one promoted the claim: "Come as you are – everyone is welcome." Two things usually prove the claim false: the sermon, and endless "opportunities" to give a gift to the church. I was looking for some kind of goofy sign to find the coffee area like, He-Brews, or Holy Grounds... I smiled when I read the sign, "Coffee Station." Before I jumped in line, I fumbled for my wallet to make a *donation*.

Some churches don't understand the image they portray by asking for people to buy their coffee. Churches appear stingy. Think about it like this, no one would believe they are welcome in your home if you ask them for a donation to cover the cost of the Folgers you serve them in a paper cup. One church I visited even tried to shame me into buying coffee, when the youth pastor stood on stage and said, "If you're bringing your own coffee to church, you should feel ashamed because you are robbing from the donations we need to fund our youth ministry."

I put my wallet away when the server said, "The coffee AND cookies are free – take as many as you'd like."

It was finally time for the service to start, so I slid into a seat in the back. The auditorium seats 4,000 people, but it always seems so intimate. The energy and excitement are palpable. People genuinely wanted to be there. It's one of the friendliest crowds I've ever been a part of. After singing a couple of songs, the pastor bounded on stage. I thought, "One line of 'pastor-speak' and I'm gone." He got up and said, "Hey! My name is Jim and I'm the pastor guy around here, but you can call me Jim." With that, he launched into his talk.

# SUCCESS PROOF

I used to think I was a pretty good preacher, until I heard this guy. He held my attention for 45 minutes. Not only did he keep me and everyone in the room engaged, he managed to help me find a fresh perspective... just about every time he spoke. I couldn't believe what was happening. I panicked as I wondered, "How am I going to keep writing the book *Success Proof* when I was finding clarity in a successful rock star church?"

Every week Jim challenged me with the truth. When I couldn't live up to the truth, he taught me how to forgive myself and find grace. His talks seemed tailored to my life.

Week after week I sat in the auditorium listening without any ministry-envy. I know I am destined to NOT be a rock star pastor. So many other pastors should give up the chase to be famous in the eyes of the Christian community. Or, stop hating the guys who have huge crowds and followings. You will end up bitter and confused. God was clearly showing me that rock stars are NOT the enemy.

What was also becoming clear is that so many guys in ministry are dying to get noticed. They will copy everything they see the big successful church rock star doing. The only thing missing from the copycat ministries of light, loud music, cool venues and slick sermons is... Jesus. Sounds judgmental, I know, but it's true.

The small church guy is just as guilty. Traditions from the past are haunting churches today. So many churches established two or three decades ago are still arguing about using words in a book or shining them on a screen. All the while condemning the mega church as the instrument of compromise and a watered down Gospel. Jesus is hard to find in those places too.

Part of the paradox for me was this: at my core I am a very simple and small ministry type, and the one place I recalibrated my life was in a rock star church. The urge to go start a successful ministry no longer tugs at my heart. Something greater is in store for me as long as I remember one thing: God wants me to be who He made me to be. Nothing more and nothing less. It's such an old concept, but so many churches and pastors are clearly ignoring it.

## A Tale of Two Jims: Jim the Grasshopper

I wouldn't trade the time I learned from rock star Jim for anything. His teaching didn't necessarily renew my faith in the big church movement. No, Jim's influence was much broader. The Gospel is for all people in all times and all places – even for rock stars who know how to handle it correctly. He also rekindled a passion deep in my spirit – to connect with people. On the other hand, it was also very frustrating to think, "No way will I ever be able to find the same thing rock star Jim has – the perfect place to completely be myself."

One of the big reasons rock star Jim is so successful is because he is only trying to be himself. I heard him express on many occasions the frustration he used to experience in other ministry contexts. In fact, it was also encouraging to hear he was on the verge of giving up in another ministry. Why? He can't be successful everywhere. So, he gave up trying to be someone else. Imagine, God wants me to be me... He wants you to be you... could I be ok with that?

I know, you are asking the same questions I did. "That sounds nice, but how can I leave what I'm doing to pursue what I believe God wants me to be? The bills need to get paid. What if I fail? What if I offend someone? What if the church doesn't grow? What if... What if..." Those questions are valid. But I think most people in ministry are dying to have the chance to be themselves. Why don't we? You can boil the excuses down to two: fear and comfort. We're afraid of losing our job and the comfort of status quo.

The hard truth is most pastors are holding out to make it to the "Major Leagues." From the outside, successful ministries look like the Promised Land. What pastor doesn't want higher pay, more recognition and the appearance of success? In most cases, it's fool's gold. I think a lot of rock star types are pressured to produce something they despise... higher numbers. One rock star type told me, "It was supposed to be the biggest night of my church's life... It was like we hit a home run when we hit the number, but my heart sunk because I knew the fence was only going to get moved back on me."

And, for the record, it's fine to be a rock star. What isn't fine is seeking status and success at any cost. Losing sight of who you are and where you have value is dangerous. You can spend your whole life in the comparison game, and never come out on the positive side of the ledger. The real giant for me, and I believe a lot of other pastors in my spot, is my own lack of confidence in thinking my contribution is enough. I'm not confused about the theology of giving it all to God and letting Him take care of the results, but we all have to find a place of real contentment.

However, chasing numbers does not satisfy or validate anyone's ministry either. The question to ask is this: what do the numbers represent? What am I really chasing? How can

I make my life's calling satisfying and earn a living? Everyone has to answer those questions for themselves. For me, I almost didn't have the courage to move past my fears... until I met Jim the grasshopper.

In the Fall of 2013, I signed up for a men's retreat with the rock star church. A lot of guys need a retreat to get charged up and refocused. Typically, I'm not one of those guys. For my whole professional life I was the one leading the events, not attending them. Besides, this retreat was two hundred bucks, and I wasn't excited enough about it to try and convince my wife we needed to spend the money. Turns out I didn't have to convince anyone.

A few days after I decided to forget about the retreat I got a phone call from a friend at the church who invited me to Starbucks. We grabbed our coffee at the counter and headed outside to chat. My friend became like an older brother to me. He could tell I was trying to figure what was "next" in my life. He opened the conversation by saying, "Let's go to the men's retreat in a couple of weeks... I'll even pay for your registration." I guess I couldn't say no to his offer. "In fact, I want you to meet a guy named Jim... no, not pastor Jim," he said grinning. "A different Jim. He's a brilliant guy, a doctor, and someone who helped organize the retreat. He might be a good person for you to connect with."

It was settled. I was going to the retreat. My only real cost was meeting a brilliant guy named Jim.

One good thing about attending rock star church retreats – they spare no expense. The setting was literally a mountain top experience. Ten thousand feet above sea level for the weekend was definitely a perk. The evening was perfect. Colorado sunsets are unrivaled in beauty. Even though I was a little apprehensive about the weekend and meeting Dr. Jim, I was soaking in the mountain top experience.

"Jason!" my friend shouted from the distance. "Come over here and meet Jim." Getting to know people in a huge church is not easy. On that weekend, I knew no one except for my friend. The church has 20,000 people, and I never saw the same person twice. So, what was about to happen was... well... miraculous.

I reached out my hand to shake Jim's. It was hard not to think about his credentials and feeling intimidated. He looked smart. Jim is about six foot four with salt and pepper hair combed neatly to one side. He has a manner of speaking that is quick and very precise. I felt really small standing there next to him. "So, how did you start attending the church?" asked Jim. I told him briefly about my former life in ministry, and that I'd been to the Northwest and back after planting a church. "The Northwest?" he grilled me. And then, he started to ask a series of questions that rocked my world.

"Wait a minute," he added, "Do you know Mega Pastor?" He knew Mega Pastor? "Yes!" I almost shouted. We looked at each other... and then we turned to my friend, and at the same time we all said, "Wow!"

My head was swimming. Turns out, our past and experiences with Mega Pastor were nearly identical. Finally, I met someone who helped me gain perspective. This may sound strange, but in a way I had some confirmation I wasn't *completely* crazy. Just learning that I wasn't the only one who went through the same ordeal lifted a tremendous burden from my mind.

We shared a similar conclusion: some people will do anything to build an empire, even at the expense of others. Jim and I knew the pain of being told, "You're not good enough." I might have believed that lie if God had not arranged for me to attend the men's conference that weekend.

It's the same lie the Israelites believed thousands of years ago. In Numbers 13:33, this is the lie, "*We even saw giants there, the descendants of Anak. Next to them we felt like grasshoppers, and that's what they thought, too!*" In other words, when you look at the successful pastors, you're nothing but a grasshopper, and your contributions in this world are nothing compared to them. Numbers 13:33 speaks to frustrated leaders (like me) who dream of shedding our grasshopper legs and one day becoming successful giants. It's not a worthy pursuit.

Dr. Jim was not a rock star in the church. He was a volunteer…some might even say a grasshopper. At the same time, his influence was incredible. The rock star church needed him to organize their events. I can't understate his value. He was not interested in gaining recognition – He was being who God called him to be.

Be who you are. Nothing more. Nothing less.

# Chapter Eight | MENTORS MATTER

## Should I Stay Or Should I Go

If you really want to be "great," work with and for someone who trusts you. Ask them, "How many mistakes can I make? How did you help the last guy reach his potential? Do you have a succession plan?" The point is, look for a mentor who will transfer their precious power.

I had no idea what I had… until I left it behind.

Three months into a new ministry, and I was beginning to feel a sense of dread. Everyone who could be visited was visited. Seriously, the church was all of 40 people. And, after the first round of calls, I wasn't eager to reschedule any more visits. Even though I like people, I get really frustrated trying to make "small talk." Not only that, but most of the people who agreed to visit with me were leery of the new "preacher." So, I did nothing but stare at the outdated church pictorial directory wondering what I should do next.

A sudden realization came over me, "This is exactly why guys leave a place like this… it's lonely… and the very people you are there to help, are a little more than skeptical about your intentions." A lot of guys in rural churches work two and three jobs to help supplement their income (and boredom). Up to this point, my experience was working in multi-staff church settings. I missed daily interactions with a team.

For the first time in my life, I entertained a dangerous thought, "I don't think ministry is for me." I was only four years into my ministry career at the time, and I was developing what one of my favorite authors calls the "quitter's gene." Once again, I believed my circumstances were impossible to deal with, so I looked for an escape. No one told me ministry was going to be like *this*. And then, I played the "if only game." If only I fought harder to stay a little longer with my first ministry... if only...

## The Greatest Mentor I Should Have Never Left

My start in ministry was as smooth as it gets. Some guys have trouble finding a place where they fit, but I was given a great opportunity right out of college. My home church was only three hundred miles south of the college I attended to study ministry. During my junior year of college, my home church began a search for a new pastor, and it couldn't have happened at a better time for me. I wasn't in line for the "throne," but I was a good candidate to take the associate position under whoever was hired. I had volunteered at the church, worked as an intern, and had deep family roots there.

When the "new guy" was hired, the church began a search for a youth pastor. Well, they named the position "Associate Pastor" to make it sound more like a real pastor job. After looking for nearly a year, and even flying a candidate in from

## SUCCESS PROOF

two states away, they were not able to fill the position. So, my home church "punted." They called me in May and asked if I could fill the spot during the summer until they found someone else in the fall. I agreed.

The first day I showed up for work as the official intern was exciting. I had a meeting with the new guy, and was a little intimidated. Andy was a pro's pro in the ministry. He was from Chicago and was all business. When I first met Andy I wasn't terribly impressed with his appearance. Seriously, he looked the part of a Midwest accountant. He wore a tie every day, carried a leather briefcase (the old school style), and had meticulously combed Jimmy Johnson style hair. No pastor in Colorado wore a tie and dress slacks to the office. So, when he invited me into his office for the first time, I wasn't sure what to expect.

"Jason, let's get a few things straight... we work six days a week because most of the people we work with have real jobs," concluded Andy. "We dress professionally around here, so that means no shorts or T-Shirts," he said calmly. And then he motioned to the door, "Most importantly, we work as a team, and as long as that door is closed, you can say anything you want. You can even disagree with me," he said soberly. "But when we go out in public, I expect solidarity... understand?" I nodded, and then snuck across the hall to consult a dictionary:

> sol·i·dar·i·ty
> noun: **solidarity**; singular proper noun: **Solidarity**;
> noun: **Solidarity**
> > 1. unity or agreement of feeling or action, especially among individuals with a common interest; mutual support within a group.

Solidarity sounded good to me. After that day, Andy no longer needed to "lay down the law." Eventually, he even loosened up and got rid of the tie for polo shirts (he never did ditch the slacks or briefcase though). We had an amazing working relationship. He was the perfect mentor for me.

Andy had a vision to be what he called a "church planting church." In other words, we would plant churches that planted other churches and one day see a great movement come from our work. As a 22 year old college graduate, I was thrilled to work under someone who wanted to change the world. In essence, Andy trusted me. He actively looked for ways to maximize my gifts. He indulged some of my crazy ideas (like allowing me to take a two month paid hiatus to visit South Africa to consider full time missionary work).

Only recently did I realize the things Andy and I accomplished together. Everything I really wanted to do in ministry was coming to pass, but I was too young and stupid to realize it. After reflecting on my experiences with the Cool Church, I started to connect a few dots. The Cool Church had all of the resources rock star money could buy – but never really got off the ground. I thought I was a total failure in the church-planting world.

The Cool Church didn't create any "buzz" or propel anyone on staff to rock star status. And then, I had an epiphany about my time with Andy in the late 90's. He helped me plant a church and it worked back then because he kept our focus on other people rather than ourselves.

Back in 1998, churches were creating "contemporary" services. Contemporary was code (to other church connois-

# SUCCESS PROOF

seurs) for: *we no longer use an organ and a piano for our music here.* Other churches that could not commit to throwing out the hymnal adapted a "blended" service. I wonder what outsiders thought when they read church signs saying, "We have a new blended service!" They probably had visions of fruit smoothies.

The time had come for our church to move into the contemporary world, and Andy asked me to lead the charge.

He handed the entire project over to me. No one had ever dared create a contemporary style of worship at the church before. The thought of moving in drums and guitars was terrifying for a lot of long time church members of a conservative church. We were adding a service unlike the two we currently offered... and Andy was allowing me to put together a band, recruit volunteers, and do the speaking. Essentially, we were creating a church within a church. We planted a successful church.

Looking back, I should have been more grateful. Even if he never did anything else for me (and he did), Andy demonstrated amazing trust in me (for no good reason). He did two things to make the project successful, and he should be a model for all aspiring leaders:

1. He stood in between the critics and me. The sort of change we were proposing was not going to sit well with the complainers. Andy was proactive in his approach, and had the unanimous support from his elder board. The one thing I did not realize at the time was this: he did all of that for my protection. If the project was successful, he really wouldn't gain

anything personally. If we failed, he would have to take on all of the criticism, and lose a lot of credibility (especially with his leaders).

2. He did not ask to be the one to dictate the kinds of change we needed to make. Andy and I discussed ideas and worked through challenges, but he allowed me to make the final decisions. You have to understand, this one change could instigate the real growth in the church. In other words, Andy was not looking to claim any credit for the one thing in his profession that receives most attention--numbers of attendees.

Yes, we encountered problems and had setbacks. Everyone does. However, not everyone has the kind of capacity that Andy does to develop talent and give away power. I didn't know how rare of a leader Andy is... until I left. Honestly, I never really had the same kind of "success" I did with him.

Andy's vision worked. As far as I could tell, he wasn't merely interested in building a personal empire. Our purpose was to reach a new and different group of people. In a matter of months the service was completely full and the main reason the church began to grow again. Sadly, I didn't recognize it for what it really was... a successful church plant.

To this day, Andy is very low-key about the success of his vision... and his investment in my life. I am fortunate to be able to travel more these days in my role as a Philanthropic Portfolio Manager, so I scheduled a time to visit with Andy on one of my trips through his town. I wanted to tell him about my theory of planting a church within a church and try to convey the difference he'd made in my life.

## SUCCESS PROOF

# Thanking an Old Friend

We met at a Wendy's close to his office – probably because it was my turn to pick up the tab. "You know what Hanselman?" he asked in his customary booming voice, "Don't you know that taking your old boss to a Wendy's is *cheap!*" Not to be outdone, I suggested, "Oh come on Andy… maybe you could re-apply and get your old job back as fry cook?" Andy let out his signature-snorting chortle (a sure sign he was genuinely amused) and said, "Which is more than I could say for you… now hurry up and pay for my coffee."

After we grabbed our drinks and eased into the plastic booth, we were able to pick right up where we'd left off months ago. We went through the normal litany of questions about our lives: family, ministry and God's favorite team (the Denver Broncos) before I decided to ask a divergent question. "Let me ask you something Andy… do you realize that your dream of becoming a church planting church actually came to pass?" Blank stare. "We did all of the things necessary to plant a church: we recruited a band, we found a space, we purchased new equipment, and we invited a whole new demographic to be a part of the church… and it was successful."

In typical fashion, Andy wasn't terribly impressed with himself. He admitted the church had made a shift in thinking, but it was the necessary course of action to continue meeting the needs of people in the community and the church. Great leaders, like Andy, are more interested in the growth of others and their organization, rather than finding accolades for themselves. As I was writing this chapter, I came across a description to summarize my point:

Those who work hardest to help others succeed will be seen by the group as the leader or the 'alpha' of the group. And being the alpha – the strong, supportive one of the group, the one willing to sacrifice time and energy so the others may gain – is a prerequisite for leadership (Simon Sinek).[7]

Maybe Andy is the "norm" for most pastors, but I doubt it. Or, it's possible he secretly desires to be a successful rock star pastor, and is still waiting for his opportunity to "get noticed." I doubt it. Why would Andy spend 40 years in ministry, more than half of them at his current position? He definitely does not power through the grind of local church ministry to get a free cup of coffee at Wendy's… at least I hope not anyway.

Leave Andy at Wendy's for a moment… and take some time with my most recent mentor – Don.

## Another Chance to Be Mentored

A few months ago I received one of those texts no one wants to read. It was from my wife, and it went something like this: "Are you sitting down? You need to know Don's wife passed away suddenly today. I'm so sorry." It was devastating to read.

Not long after, we sat in a church building and wept through the service for Don's wife. I was amazed again to hear about the rich relationship Don enjoyed with his wife of 30 years. Don's favorite line has always been, "She spoiled me and was better to me than I deserved." As the stories flowed during the

---

7  Sinek. (2014). <u>Leaders Eat Last: Why Some Teams Pull Together and Others Don't.</u> (New York: Penguin Group)

funeral service I had a profound thought as I glanced over at my wife, "I want to be the next Mr. & Mrs. Don."

Don gave to others out of the satisfying relationship he enjoyed at home, and I am one of the many who benefitted from their relationship.

Rewind the tape three years prior to the funeral. Shortly after I was laid off from the Cool Church position, the Bell Church invited me to preach. After my second or third Sunday, I received an invitation to "friend" someone through one of my social media networks. The name was not familiar to me, but after reading his biographical information, I was impressed. He held an MA, was a manager at a technology company for a long time, and was very well connected.

"*Who is this guy*? And why would he ever want to connect with me?"

## Lunch With Don

I quickly discovered how well loved Don was by just about everyone at the Bell Church. Even though I really thrive on meeting new people and building relationships, I was a little skeptical. My recent experience told me that everyone has an agenda – especially the well-connected church guy type. Reluctantly, I set up a time to meet him for lunch – if nothing else; at least I could get a free lunch.

I got to the restaurant five minutes late (secretly hoping he might leave before I got there). After a quick survey of the room, I couldn't locate anyone who fit the profile of a well-educated technology guru. The only person who flagged me down was guy in a plaid shirt, blue jeans and a tattered hat. He kind of looked like Francis Schaeffer with gray balding hair and a goatee. No turning back now. He'd spotted me and was waiving me over to the table.

"Don?" I asked with hesitation. He grinned and shook my hand. "Sit down," as he passed me a menu. "Get whatever you want... I'm buying." Five minutes into our conversation I knew I had hit the jackpot. "I don't want anything from you, and you are free to tell me to butt out whenever you want," he said. "You can't hurt my feelings, so just be yourself."

He's one of the few people to ever tell me to be myself... and I am forever grateful.

Some people have impressive credentials on paper, but this guy knew his stuff. We had a real conversation about life, ministry and hatching schemes to conquer the world. It was refreshing to meet a person who listened. He *really* was interested in my crazy ideas. Even though very few of those ideas ever got off the ground, Don was always connecting me to people and resources to get me help.

My admiration for him grew as I watched him live out his faith in a real way. Lots of church leaders talk about helping people, but Don actually did something. I marveled at how he targeted people with "messy lives"... like Dave and Bill (not their real names) or as most people at church referred to them as "the twins." Dave and Bill were thirty-somethings with developmental disabilities who attended the church. They were awkward and didn't "play church" like the rest of us. Every week, one of "the twins" would blurt out, "Blood of Christ!" right before drinking his grape juice during communion.

# SUCCESS PROOF

If you were new to the church, it might be a little unnerving to hear someone shouting something unintelligible about blood. Of course, the very religious in the crowd were offended and would grumble to me after service. "Why are *they* (never using Bill and Dave's names) so noisy during the Lord's Supper?!" In my best "pastor-speak" voice I would *gently* suggest, "If only we all could respond like *they* do… as though this were our very first time taking communion," and then bow my head and move away slowly. I know… not a very mature attitude. But come on, it was funny. Every week, someone was startled awake by Dave and Bill's outburst. Even funnier were the utter contempt on the faces of some of the Sunday regulars.

Some people scoffed at them, others laughed, but Don reached and really helped.

One afternoon during the week, Don pulled into the church lot with "the twins" crammed into his tiny Toyota pick up. He jumped out and bounded to the door. "Wow!" Don exclaimed. "Those guys can really eat!" He told us that he had been working outside with "the twins" all morning, and then took them to lunch. "You've been working with them, *and you fed them?*" I asked. "Yep… we had some yard work I needed to get done," Don added. "They needed work this week, so I invited them to help… and they were hungry too."

Anyone who would spend the afternoon with those two guys, and then offer to pay for their lunch is an extraordinary person. Essentially, Don was providing adult day care. No one asked him to do it. No one paid him. They needed work, and he helped them find it for the day. He just saw needs, and met them. Beautiful.

## Not Impressed

To set the record straight, Andy and Don are not impressed with me. They saw some potential and did their best to extract it. And, neither of them is a perfect saint. Not every decision they made was perfect (and if either of them ever read this, they will disagree). My intent is not to glamorize my mentors, but to give some strong advice. This may be the only section of this book where I tell you what to do. Why? This one area of ministry is critical, and will shape your thinking about your career in ministry more than anything else. It's all about people, and that includes the PEOPLE you CHOOSE to work for and with. Be wise. Take heed. Listen to all the words of warning.

## More Greatness Thoughts

Andy and Don were able to do something most other guys in the Baby Boomer generation refuse to do – trust and empower. Before you think I am saying we should dump everyone over sixty from church leadership, just take a deep breath. I'm asking younger pastors and leaders to make wiser choices. Some leaders cannot change. It's not "in them" to help you grow and develop. In fact, some of them will always be micromanaging freaks.

I'll repeat what I said in the opening lines of this chapter:

> *If you really want to be great, work with and for someone who trusts you. ... look for a mentor who will transfer their precious power.*

# SUCCESS PROOF

Andy had a lot on the line, but he handed over some of his authority to get the job done. You will work harder for someone who treats you like an adult.

Pay close attention to the way the leader treats people who can never repay them. I started to think back to my short time at Cool Church. Initially, it felt great to be on the "inside" because I was convinced we were all that – and a bag of chips. When the church did not grow, things began to change. It became very clear I was expendable when I could not get Mega Pastor where he wanted to be in life. It felt like I was only around to make his dream come true. There's no other way to say this – that brand of leadership sucks.

Don could not have been more different. He lives to make other people's dreams come true. He has an attitude of abundance and not scarcity. No one wonders if Don has ulterior motives – he spent time with people, like "the twins", who could never repay him. Authenticity is more than a church buzzword. Watch your mentor closely and *judge their actions*. If they are the real deal like Don, hang in there with them. If not, find the eject button and bail.

I know this sounds so self-evident. It's not. I ignored everything I knew about integrity to work for Mega Pastor, keep a job and well… and do a few other things I don't want to admit. Don't be fooled – *"Wisdom is proven right by her children (Luke 7:35)."*

# Chapter Nine | BORED MEETINGS, BAD BOSSES & NEW BEGINNINGS

## The Unavoidable Subject

Up to this point, I've managed to avoid the worn out topic of elders, board of directors, deacons, and any other reference to church hierarchy. This may be the one area where the rock star pastors have the biggest advantage over the garden-variety pastor. Most rock star types get to set the tone, call the shots and create. Granted, many of them have earned the right to lead, but few pastors in small churches are ever given the freedom to make decisions. Let's take a short dive back into the bitter side of ministry for a moment because it represents the brightest spot in my career.

## Breathing the Same Air

A friend of mine once described church leadership as a group of people who like to breathe their own air. Somehow they manage to survive after years of doing things poorly. No matter how hard a pastor may try, it is impossible to kill a bad board. For me, board meeting were like episodes of **The Walking Dead**. You would make a decision after a two hour meeting only to come back the next month to hash through it all over again... for another two hours. When I was working for a church, I didn't have much compassion for the blatant incompetence.

So, incompetence is a little too harsh. Most people appointed to leadership positions in church are not trained or shown how to lead. They are recruited with a line that goes something like this, "We've noticed your commitment to this church (translation: you come to Sunday service at least two times a month), and we would be honored if you would serve as an elder. Now, it won't take much time or work on your part, but we believe you're the right fit for the job." It's flattering – sort of, but anyone who agrees to that kind of proposal is (for obvious reasons) not suited to serve as a leader.

I know the guy in the middle of Nebraska or Kansas is going to argue, "But we didn't really have anyone to choose from." I really do understand, and am not being overly critical. However, I am tired of excuses to settle for second best, or the lazy way out of finding creative leadership solutions. When you take the easy way out you get a group of guys who are NOT eager to do something great, but a pack of people who want to preserve the peace – and the air in the room turns poisonous.

## My Final Board Meeting

Three years removed from my final church board meeting and it is still fresh in my mind. It was a meeting that almost didn't happen. We had a habit of finding last minute excuses for cancelling meetings. Most times, I would welcome the cancellation because I could invest my two hours into something more productive – like catching up on the last three episodes of Breaking Bad on Netflix.

For the first time ever, I was eager for the meeting to happen. Tension in the church was mounting. The finance committee was angry with the elder board over (what else) money. In fact, the head of the finance committee stopped sending me the financial reports as an act of defiance. Little did he know I was relieved I didn't have to read through 10 pages of bad reporting and numbers. No one could ever boil the numbers down to a readable and coherent document.

We spent more time putting out fires and lamenting the complaints of people who could never be satisfied. The usual complaints, "When is the organ coming back?" "Why is the music so loud?" "Why doesn't the pastor wear a suit and tie?" My patience wore thin. No one wanted to really lead. So, I hatched a plan to force a decision.

This church faced the same dilemma a lot of other dysfunctional churches face: a dwindling bank account. My hunch was that the church was going to lay off staff to "solve the money problem." It was a sneaky tactic. Our youth group had *grown* from twenty to ten in the past three years, and they wanted to re-engineer the pastoral staff. It's easier to spin a layoff than it is for the board to come right out and say you are going to fire someone. They knew the highest value for many of the people attending the church was to see money in the bank. In an effort to keep the church afloat financially, they would have no other recourse but to cut a salary and hope one day God would bless enough to help them rehire.

# SUCCESS PROOF

The move is clever and wrong on so many levels. If the leaders were not happy with someone's performance, tell them. Some guys will rise to the occasion and turn things around. If the situation doesn't improve, you have at least given that person an opportunity to grow. Also, the move makes God responsible for the church's demise in finances. "IF God blesses us…" translates: God is responsible. The real issue is bad leadership, and they needed to own it.

Go back and re-read chapter two. No one should ever be patronized with the line, "Well, we don't have enough money, so we're going to have to lay you off." I knew it was a lie. The guy at this church would know it was a lie. I was not going to be a part of another cowardly church fiasco.

My final question to the board that night was this, "Is this really a financial decision we're talking about tonight – yes or no?" The answer, after much hemming and hawing was, "Yes." I said, "In that case, I'm resigning… and all of your money problems are solved."

I was done with wasting my time and life in a dysfunctional leadership environment.

## The Plan

Let me go back three months before this scene. The hand wringing over money was getting way more air time in our meetings than necessary. Instead of talking about transformation and ministry, we were diving into a worthless pile of numbers (of which I was not receiving in advance of meetings). I even went as far to say, "I really don't think I need to attend these meetings anymore – the greatest impact of my work is seen on Sundays, not in here talking about things that do not matter." Yep. I said that. And no, it did not win me any allies in the boardroom.

If money was the problem, what could we do? My plan was simple. Instead of one person getting axed, all staff members could take a half cut in pay. I liked the fact that it was unilateral, and didn't single out any one staff member. In order to take a pay cut, I would need another job to survive. I wanted to start a church in a neighboring city that would meet on Thursday nights. Starting a Thursday night church would not be easy, but it had some definite advantages:

1. It wouldn't interfere with Sunday morning.
2. I would look for outside sources for funding.
3. The church could solve their money problem.
4. No one would get laid off.
5. The church could double its influence in the surrounding community.

To pitch the idea, I put together a 15-page plan (cool graphics and everything) and presented it to one of the church elders over lunch. He wasn't impressed. In fact, what I didn't know was that he scheduled a "secret" meeting with the other elders to come up with a rebuttal in advance of the monthly meeting. Their objections were flimsy to me:

- What if someone needs to see you in an emergency?
- We don't want you serving two masters.

Disappointing to say the least. I could count on one hand the number of "emergencies" requiring immediate attention in my career. I'm not even sure what that would look like.

And, the reference to serving two masters is laughable. In truth, I was trying to serve the SAME master TWICE as hard.

Was my plan the best? Probably not. It was something new and creative. Maybe that's why it never got off the ground. I knew my days were numbered. My inability to accept their decision forced me to think about changing my focus in ministry. I could not get over the fact that the church leadership would rather ruin someone's life rather than looking for a creative option.

## You Mad Bro?

Yes, I was angry at the church. I convinced myself my anger was righteous, but I just was a bad fit in an ineffective church. Even if I had good reasons to leave, one of the hardest things to do in the world is to convince other pastors and churches you aren't a church wrecker. If you've had a couple of short-term ministries, you know what I'm talking about. The deepest wounds have come from leaders of churches where I no longer serve. My most heart breaking moments have come at the hands of "mature Christian" leaders.

Dan was one of the worst examples. He was a member of the leadership team for the Cool Church I worked with. With all of the money and expertise invested in that project, someone needed to be held responsible for the disappearing money and low numbers of people attending. The Cool Church was not a success story. When I was asked to leave, the leadership team needed to spin a story about why I had to go. After all, they made the decision and needed to justify their reasons.

Enter Dan. He was a middle-aged guy working for a big church in the same region as the Cool Church. He was from corporate America, made lots of money, and made a career shift to ministry. He was an "obvious" choice for leadership. The problem was, Dan knows virtually nothing about leading and building a ministry. For some reason, Dan saw it as his duty to sully my name in the community. You might wonder, "Why are you doing the same thing?" Great question. I'm comfortable telling Dan's story because I actually took the time to confront him face to face with a witness.

In a matter of weeks after my lay off, Dan was busy telling potential employers (a.k.a. churches) I was not worthy of hire for three reasons: (1) I split a church; (2) I was "redirecting" or stealing money from the Cool Church; (3) I have bad character. No words can describe the depth of my anger when I heard his accusations. Call me a lot of things, but Dan was way off on all three of these charges. So, I took my wife with me and went to his office when I learned what he was saying.

The reality is, Dan never worked directly with me. I still have no idea what Dan does in his current position – except sit on boards and make accusations about innocent people. We knocked on his office door, sat across from him at his desk, and asked him to explain his accusations. He said, "You took people with you when you left… money stopped coming the day you were laid off… and Mega Pastor told me you are not willing to complete projects he assigned you." Point by point we refuted his talking points, and then I asked him, "Now that you've heard my side of the story, what do you have to say for yourself?"

# SUCCESS PROOF

Picture a fifty something year old man, in a white dress shirt, who stands over six feet tall. I'm only five foot eight and a buck seventy and change in weight. Dan towers over me in height and weight… but not that day. He sulked behind his desk and trembled as we looked him in the eye and demanded an answer. Maybe no one had ever dared to challenge him before, but cowards like Dan always shrink back in adversity.

"I still think you're a bad guy," Dan said.

My answer was direct, "Then shame on you… I'm assuming you know what Matthew 18 teaches (pretty sure he had no idea). Jesus gives clear instructions on how to handle confrontation," I went on "At least I was man enough to come look you in the eye and confront you… a man of your age and position should be ashamed."

And we left him sweating and quaking in his over-sized office chair. Dan never apologized for slandering my character. I suppose his position is more important to him than his relationship with God and other believers.

I was angry with church leaders for a long time after that, and I wish I would have settled the matter before I tried to move on with my life. Leaning on past grievances and only looking to bad examples of Christian leadership drove me to depression. Deep down I know people like Dan do not represent real Christianity. Why do they affect me so much? I needed a breakthrough. But first, I would have to endure another difficult trial before I would see the light at the end of the tunnel.

JASON HANSELMAN

# Micromanagers

My anger led me to do what any respectable pastor would do – run! I was convinced churches were the only non-profit organizations led by poor leaders and ineffective boards. Go ahead...call me naïve. The next organization I worked for was almost worse. I believed the founder when he said, "Our financials are great, we have been around for 30 years, and we just want to go to the next level." I trusted him and agreed to work as their fundraiser.

Most of what he said was true. The financials had been good, but they leveled off and were beginning to decline because of a dwindling donor base. No one was willing to make some changes and find new donors. Our return on direct mailers was less than one percent... and the pressure to perform was mounting after only six months.

My boss was the world's worst micromanager. He told me I was free to operate, but he was never happy when I wouldn't do things "his way." Every Monday morning was our staff meeting time... and every Monday morning he would remind me of my failure. I was beginning to think I was cursed. God brought me out of ministry and into another situation where I could not win. And, this new boss was doing his very best to kill my self-esteem. When I tell you I was looking for a way out, I don't mean in the change jobs kind of way out. I was depressed enough to leave planet earth.

Now, I was angry with God.

I've already mentioned this, but I was working for a company that provided counseling to pastors who had been burned in ministry. The help I needed was literally sitting across the

# SUCCESS PROOF

hall from me, but I couldn't afford his help. Mostly, I couldn't afford to admit I needed his help. It was kind of cruel to work with a bunch of counselors and not be able to access their services.

And then, God showed up in my Apple email box.

You have to understand the complete irony in this story. Let me lay out the scenario. I was raising money for a Christian organization with the mission of helping pastors get counseling. I was a wounded pastor who could not admit to needing help. My boss was a control freak who never approved of my work. God sent me an email. Well, not literally, but that's how I see it. I was invited to attend a conference in Aspen, Colorado.

Perhaps my micromanaging boss could even sense the downward spiral of my psyche. Anyone who knew me would be able to tell in an instant that I was down and feeling trapped. So, I needed something to help me get a new perspective.

Truthfully, I didn't want to attend another conference, but the main speaker was famed photographer John Fielder, and it was in the mountains of Colorado during the Fall. If nothing else, I could get some time away from the tyrant and meet one of my favorite photo artists. My only hope of going was to win the scholarship contest advertised in the email from God.

Before I got permission to attend, I wrote for the scholarship. Two or three weeks later the organizers of the event wrote back and said I'd won the scholarship. Uh oh... how am I going to tell the micromanager I won a scholarship to a conference in Aspen where my company would need to pay for the hotel room? Finally, I got the courage to walk into his office and tell him the good news.

He was actually enthusiastic. "Of course!" he exclaimed. "As a matter of fact I helped create that event 30 years ago…" What?! If I didn't think God sent me the email before, I was definitely convinced now. Two small miracles in a row! I packed and left for Aspen a week later with no real intentions on learning anything new or exciting. I did make up my mind I was going to meet John Fielder.

Fielder gave the first talk of the day. I was fascinated by his photos from places all over the world. And during the first break I was inspired to go out and take some photos of my own. I strolled up a hill and past a huge Suburban parked on the side of the road as I looked for the "perfect shot." The door of the SUV creaked open and John Fielder appeared. "Hey… I'm John," he said. "You can get a better look at that if you go down this path and to the other side." Miracle number three – photo advice from John Fielder!

I took a great photo and got back to the sessions. Little did I know, the real miracle of the weekend was still to come. God never does anything small.

After my encounter with Fielder, I wandered into the first open door where I slid into a seat at the back to take in a workshop. Could it get any better? Yes. I was about to meet a man who would act as the catalyst for the most significant change in my professional career. Jay the Catalyst was the real reason I was in Aspen.

The Catalyst launched into his presentation, and he caught my attention right away. He rocked an old school flip chart with markers and his own handwriting – such a refreshing change from the PowerPoint robots I would listen to later in the day. Jay was describing a process I only dreamed about using where I worked... but knew my boss would never accept it. Jay never mentioned how to write letters or how to host another "rubber chicken" event.

The light broke through the darkness, and I have never been the same since.

The session ended and the subject matter literally made me forget all about John Fielder. I waited my turn in line to talk with the Catalyst. Finally, I got to the front and asked, "How can I learn more about this... it's everything I've wanted to do, but have never been allowed." I stopped short of begging for a job. He gave me his card and said, "We can get together sometime and talk." His title was President of Big Important Company. While I appreciated the gesture, I was pretty sure someone of his caliber would never have time to meet with me.

When I returned from the conference, I sent an email to Jay right away... and waited... for two weeks. I landed a meeting with him after sending two more emails and leaving a couple of voice messages. I'm persistent that way. At 12:30 in the afternoon, we met at a seafood place in the middle of Denver. It was Jay, a salmon dinner and me. He spent an hour with me going over much of what he said at the seminar. In fact, a lot of what he told me that day are things I rely on to this day for my current fundraising job.

After sixty minutes he finally said, "Look, you need to go to the people who taught me how to use these principles. Their two day workshop is not cheap, but it's worth every penny."

That's when I slumped a little in my chair and complained, "No way my boss will ever do that Jay." And then he asked, "Let me send an email or call… what's his name?" I told him and he raised his eyebrows. "I worked with him 20 years ago – I'm sure he'll listen to me."

And now I realize the God-sized path I was traveling. God had not left me. No one could possibly take the mess I was in and make it right – except for God. In spite of my bad choices, angry disposition and raging depression, God was doing something amazing. The final miracle was Jay picking up the tab for the expensive lunch.

Well, maybe the greatest miracle is how Jay convinced my boss to pay $3000 for the two-day training he told me about that day over lunch..

## New Beginnings

I'm still struggling with the idea of church boards – well, at least how they are currently structured. Can a group of middle aged white guys who are breathing the same air lead well? Yes, but it may be in spite of themselves. Eventually, enough normal guys like me will look to other places and organizations in the Kingdom that want to do more than keep a tight reign on the status quo. God needed to work an absolute miracle in my life for me to have hope again. As I reflect on the "older" guys in my life like Jay the Catalyst, Andy, Don and Jim the Grasshopper who are forward in their thinking, I believe there is hope in this world for something new.

Perhaps the only way for any of us to realize something better is to experience pain. I realize I don't deserve to be rescued or given anything. My attitude was to be angry at God and almost throw in the towel. I want to take one more chapter to look backward, and then finish by sharing more about my new beginning in ministry.

# Chapter Ten | THE IMPACT OF SMALL CHURCHES

Ministry is a paradox. The places you will sometimes find the greatest impact will also be the ones to bring the most pain. Sometimes, the pain gives you a new appreciation for a path you might have never decided to walk. I certainly wasn't looking to spend much time in places I used to call "backwards." One small decision makes a huge difference. Would I go back and make different choices if I could? Five years ago, I would have easily said, "Yes!" Today, I'm not so sure. Even though some of the small ministries I chose to be a part of were painful and sometimes hard, the risk had a lot of reward.

I know now that my choices were perfectly designed to keep me far away from rock star status… forever. Very few graduates have a well thought out life plan. Who am I kidding? Fewer than ten percent even have a plan, and even fewer have one that is any good. I just decided to move in a direction, as a result, my path created certain kinds of opportunities and shaped my career forever.

## Welcome to No Name U!

My college career began in the lively, cultural center of downtown Denver, Colorado. Hanging out with tens of thou-

# SUCCESS PROOF

sands of students (all of us strangers) in the middle of a vibrant urban area energizes me. Something changed my heart in the middle of the city in my first year of college. For the first time in my life I began to see people as people, but I was also frustrated that I had no clue about how to reach out to them and talk about spiritual things. So, I made a seismic shift – I moved away from the city. In the middle of my Freshman year of college I transferred to a school (with less than 100 students) I'd never seen in the middle of rural America.

The only word to describe the campus was: unimpressive. Actually, I didn't know if I should laugh or cry. I parked my car next to a single three-story building. It wasn't a modern facility like the University of Phoenix builds. No sir. It looked like a rectangular box of bricks straight out of the 60s. As I walked through the bitter cold and wind to the front door, I actually had to sidestep a sidewalk auction (complete with an auctioneer). Uh oh Toto… I think we're in Kansas. Actually, it was Nebraska, and I was experiencing full blown culture shock.

Most people would turn around, get in their car, and go back home. Not me. I stayed. I completed a four-year degree in ministry… and I had the best time of my life. How is that possible? I soon realized you don't really need to be a rock star to make a difference.

Anyone who chooses No Name U should take a long hard look at his or her decision – especially when the college is not recognized as a "quality" institution. At the ripe old age of 19, I did not realize the ramifications of my decision. In twenty years, my professional resume sent a message I did not want it to send. Large churches will not take a second look at a guy from a graduating class of six. Even though I have as much potential and talent as others, I know I didn't have a shot at prestigious roles.

At first, I was bothered. In fact, I was angry with that 19 year-old kid for making such a stupid decision. How dare he make a reckless choice and ruin my professional career?

Maybe I could have chosen a bigger school, or transferred to one where the cool churches would at least give me a second look – but would I really be happy? I know now that my time at a Rural American Bible College was one of the best things to ever happen to me. Who knows if the education was as good as any other school... it's the people I met along the way, and the experiences I wouldn't trade. My life and path are not worse for graduating from No Name U.

Mostly, I gained an appreciation for people groups all over the world. No Name seemed to attract the kids who were non-traditional and not interested in the typical college experience. I gravitated to the ones who were serious about ministry and had a global view.

The people who come out of a place like No Name U that make a difference in the world remind me of anti-hero types in movies. In the church culture, they are people like Rich Mullins, Keith Green and others who are constantly asking, "Why?" They make you uncomfortable, but it's a good kind of uncomfortable. I was fortunate to have spent time with a few super anti-hero types during my time at No Name U. One in particular helped me develop some key ideas for this book.

We called him China Boy. He was a missionary's kid from Hong Kong. At the time, his appearance was edgy. He had long wavy hair he would either slick back into a ponytail or let it spring into an afro when it was dry. China Boy wore horned rim glasses, combat boots and flannel shirts long before they were cool. He had the sharpest and most brilliant mind I'd ever encountered, and he somehow ended up at No Name U.

His appearance screamed anti-hero, and his life matched. Most guys who graduate from Bible College are in search of a church they can grow. What did China Boy do? After graduation, he cut the ponytail off and moved back to China. He was one of the few guys who wasn't interested in becoming a rock star – he was just interested in being used. I'll let him tell you in his own words:

> God works mysteriously, meaning we can't see the big picture. We are moved around or move ourselves around as we see best or for the wrong reasons or for the right, getting our panties in a twist trying to figure out the why and where and what-all. Meanwhile, God uses us in spite of ourselves, in spite of our best intentions, in spite of our sin, … which is hopefully of some comfort to those of us who are seeking His kingdom and His righteous. I do my best (at least that's my goal), I let God do the rest and I sleep better (most) nights.

Those are good words for people (like me) who desire greatness over God.

## Farmsworth

Experience is easy to find in a rural setting, but it's not going to be glamorous – not even a little bit. A friend of mine was pastoring a church 30 miles outside of town, and he wanted someone to come with him and work with the older kids at his church. I agreed to come with him and check it out.

We drove for what seemed like an eternity to a tiny town in the middle of Farmsworth USA. The drive to the church took us by a small feedlot complete with all of the sites and smells of living on a ranch. I would see more cows standing in a field than I would people in the community. No one was moving in, or moving out. Unless you count the cows that would soon occupy someone's dinner plate at the end of cattle season.

"Welcome to the country, city boy," said my friend as we went through the wooden doors on the white stucco building. When you first go into the doors of an older church building, the smell is always the same – mothballs. It's a scent that lingers in the air, and never leaves. I got the 10-minute tour of the little building that had stain glass windows, old wooden pews and blue carpet from the 70s. The "teen room" had a beautiful red shag carpet (the lava lamp was nowhere to be seen).

"So, how many kids come on a Sunday," I asked nervously. My friend laughed, "It depends! We always have at least one, and on a good day we'll have four." The youth program was clearly booming. "For today, I can introduce you to the kids, and then you can start teaching next week… if you come back," he said. Four awkward looking teens showed up to greet me. Two large Hispanic boys shuffled through the door -- each outweighing me by 75 pounds. My friend introduced us, but they barely even looked up or acknowledged my presence. Their sister, and another teen girl filed into the room and greeted me the same way.

# SUCCESS PROOF

Why would these four kids sit in an eight by ten room with wood paneling and shag carpet from a bygone era week after week? More importantly, how was I going to connect with them? Was this really happening?

Of course, none of those questions are the proper ones to ask. I was still thinking about me. My focus was in the wrong place. For the record, most churches and pastors have the wrong focus. A lot of us pastor types think if we can just be the most interesting guy in the universe, and have the best crafted lesson (full of dogma, doctrine, and other ugly "D" words) everything will work beautifully. And, if your students do not interact with you, then they must be at fault.

If I'd bothered to walk with them to their house after church, I would have understood what they really need. Those kids were living in absolute poverty... and I'm not only talking about their financial condition. I wanted to give them "sound doctrine", and that's not a bad thing. I'm sure the message of a good and loving God didn't penetrate their hearts because they were experiencing something less than the careful attention of a good God. In other words, God probably seemed distant and not very good at all.

Depressed economic areas like Farmsworth are limited in the kinds of people they can attract. Contrast that with cool churches that get started in population centers where upwardly mobile professionals live. A very engaging speaker is hired to assemble an amazing team to attract people who can help the church become self-sustaining. I get the economics behind it. However, it leaves little room for people like me. My first lesson and sermon at Farmsworth was... well... awful. My cool church boss would have said, "You just don't have the 'face for this place (and yes, that's a real quote).'"

Let me say this again, large churches and "relevant" churches have their place. My contention is that they are not as effective, on a per capita basis, of shaping new leaders. Farmsworth, and hundreds of other churches like it, have helped hundreds of young men and women get their start in ministry. Cool churches want someone already proven to come and help lead. I am still amazed at the willingness of Farmsworth to put up with my sub-par teaching so that I could learn the trade of ministry.

Instead of impacting one local church, they have influenced thousands of people worldwide. Just to know someone believes in you, and is willing to invest in you is a powerful thing. Sadly, not even I fully appreciated the investment made in my own life because I was too busy asking the wrong questions.

Everyone (and I mean everyone) gets a chance to do *something* at Farmsworth... but only a handful of really gifted people are afforded the privilege of standing on stage in a cool church. This doesn't mean every church should install shag carpet and move to places where nobody lives. However, Farmsworth has a lot to teach us about empowering people and less about creating a great experience on Sunday mornings. Guess which one is more lasting? I never became a rock star, but I was given the chance to grow. Someone trusted me enough to give me a chance, and that was enough.

## SUCCESS PROOF

# The Lone Ranger Church

My Lone Ranger ministry was the best and worst of experiences. As the only person on staff, I did my best to pastor a group of people who were steeped in tradition. Many of the changes I wanted to make, and some of the ones I actually did make, always caused a stir among the elders. Even simple changes, like the order of the worship service on Sunday morning, was more than some of them could handle. But I forged ahead with change because I was impatient and wanted to get results.

I don't even remember the things I fought so hard for either. Not many of the church folks cared anyway. The church had been around for almost 80 years and weathered a lot of "fancy church growth" ideas from the pastors in the past. Somehow, I managed to get along with most of the people in spite of my meddling. Not all churches are meant to explode in growth – especially when the town was only 1300 people. Instead of building a massive church, something much better happened.

The people of the church welcomed us and made my children feel safe and loved. We spent seven years in the community – three on staff at the church followed by four happy years as regular attendees. Our family grew from three to five during those years. Lone Ranger Church excelled at loving our family. They encouraged my kids to be themselves – especially when it made them laugh.

Usually, my kids were at their "best" on stage during the annual Christmas play. One year, my middle child insisted she wear her sunglasses to church and wore them during the entire play. Her teachers thought it was hilarious that one of the holy angels wore shades.

The next year, my son got the part of the baby Jesus. Right in the middle of the performance, he decided to crawl out of the manger. Of course, no one stopped him... they encouraged him to keep crawling.

If the people secretly spoke poorly of our children, we never knew it. Believe me, my kids gave them plenty of ammunition. Like the time my son helped himself to a fistful of the offering on stage one Sunday morning. I jumped up and had a little wrestling match with him... on stage... prying the money out his little hands. I was mortified. Everyone else roared in laughter. We had some good moments and memories to share.

And then, there were the things that had us wondering what was wrong with those people. The Lone Ranger church is located in the middle of Nebraska sugar beat country where the wind blows non-stop in sub-zero temperatures. When it was winter, we froze. In the summer, we baked. Of course the church had no control over the weather conditions, but the parsonage we had to live in was not a good shelter for human beings. Living in that pit was enough to cause a lot of strife in our home.

Sometimes we would invite people over for "prayer meetings" on Monday nights during football season. My favorite team was the Denver Broncos, so needless to say, we did a lot of praying. During one game in December we invited someone to watch the game with us. The wind and cold were especially bad that night, and my friend looked over at me during a commercial and asked, "Why do you have the windows open in winter?!"

# SUCCESS PROOF

The parsonage didn't have any storm windows, and the ones we did have were porous. I moved the curtain back and he saw the shrink film was bowing inwardly as the wind pressed against it. He said, "Wow! How do you stay warm at night?" The kids wore their snowsuits to bed sometimes, and we all wore stocking caps and several layers.

If it were just the windows, that would be understandable. Shortly after we moved out we discovered why our middle child was always sick. The mold behind the walls was so bad that the house had to be condemned and razed. Those memories are not so good.

How could such a friendly group of people expect us to live in such a pitiful home? The paradox was mind-boggling. Maybe no one before us had ever complained. I sincerely doubt that. I really think it boiled down to a group of leaders who did not want to jeopardize the status quo. Sacred cows, like parsonages, have sentimental meaning to church folk. Getting rid of an icon might have been costly – both in finances and in emotional strain. So, they simply did nothing while we lived there.

At the end of a three-year ministry with the church, we moved half an hour west of the church to a larger town. We also begged them to consider selling the property and buying something better for the next family who ministered there. And to their credit, they purchased a much nicer place for the new preacher. The next four years I moved into a different leadership role with another organization, but we kept attending the church. When the next pastor came, the church really grew under his leadership. My wife and kids were grateful we did not have to find a new church and try to fit into a new community.

Not many pastors in rural communities who leave a church are welcomed back. The church leaders asked me to remain in leadership and be a valuable member of their team. I was happy to stay.

No one is ever going to hear about the Lone Ranger church for three reasons: (1) it's not on the way to anywhere important, (2) it has no rock star leaders, and (3) it's the kind of ministry most guys use as a stepping-stone. Few churches are as good at loving kids and families like that one. Rural communities are often plagued with drug abuse and crime among teenagers. The Lone Ranger church prevented a lot of kids from straying from their faith because of a few very committed volunteers who were active in the lives of their youth. Children were loved and accepted.

The church growth experts will tell you that large churches are the most viable option for families because they can provide options and choices for a family. Honestly, my family doesn't need one more thing to do during the week at church. We're busy enough. The Lone Ranger church was one of the few places where I knew my kids were loved. They knew their teachers and had a strong bond with them and the other children. No rock star church has ever been able to match the level of trust we found there. Some small churches can be effective – even when they're in the middle of a cornfield in Nebraska.

## 20 Years of Hindsight

Twenty years after graduating, I need to share two things I learned about education in a small college. No Name U, and other schools like it, are not really looking for new and better ways of doing ministry. The first thing I came to understand is that they largely exist to preserve an academic tradition. You are not supposed to think new thoughts, but to champion yesterday's dogma.

The ramifications are many. For instance, names on churches mean something to the No Name U faithful. It means they can be comfortable sending "their" students to "their" churches. So, the unintended impact of No Name U is confined to a small region full of "our churches". The outside world recognizes it as parochial, but the No Name U die-hards find great comfort in knowing they will not be infiltrated with a polluted doctrine.

My eyes were also opened to the fact that just about anyone can get into schools like No Name U. Many colleges like No Name U are desperate to attract students who want to go into full time ministry as a career. Why? The demand is dwindling for graduates from schools like No Name U. A lot of churches are hiring staff from within because they are not satisfied with the caliber of the 23-year-old graduates from smaller Bible colleges. Even though some of the people emerging with a degree from a place like No Name U, they have no business leading a church.

I understand how the under-qualified manage to matriculate. Colleges want to prop up graduation numbers, so they allow unqualified pastors to earn a degree. This in turn hinders the development of many churches that only hire graduates from "their" college. Just because a person has a degree, many church boards assume they are qualified. After the pastor is hired, it takes about a year and a half for the 1000 Honeymoon cycle to initiate.

## JASON HANSELMAN

Looking back, I also did not realize the only places I could find work was in small rural churches. Do rural churches need good pastors? Yes! Just be prepared to be in a culture that is not ready for change, neither is it suited for growth (because you will work in a place with fewer than 20,000 people). I may not be perfectly suited for small, rural ministry....but I have some great stories from those places.

# Chapter Eleven | BETTER THAN A ROCK STAR

*"And he is the head of the body, the church. He is the beginning, the firstborn from the dead, that in everything he might be preeminent."* **Colossians 1:12**

Some people come into your life and completely rock your world. My universe got turned upside down one bitterly cold December night. We'd (a group of about eight) just left one of the hookiest "honky-tonk" bars in north Denver. No, we weren't there for the drink because we weren't old enough. As hard as this is to admit, we were there to line dance. Three hours of "Boot Scoot Boogie", neon lights, and a lot of urban cowboys. I didn't want to be anywhere else in the world.

The dancing and Alan Jackson music was nice, but I had another motive… true love. That's right. I was a sucker for a beautiful brown-eyed girl who was actually interested in me. While the rest of our crew was busting a move to the Cotton Eye Joe, my new romantic interest and I were deep in conversation.

No one had ever captivated my attention like this – no one.

I barely heard the chatter from the others in our group when we left, "Look at the love-birds," my friends chided. "It's time to go already, didn't you notice the music isn't playing?" We didn't. The conversation continued as we threw on our winter coats and headed out into the cold night air.

The four of us squeezed into the front seat of my cowboy friend's car. The brown land barge was my affectionate name for his car that seated four people comfortably – in the front seat. I sat close to the brown-eyed girl and waited for her to continue the story of her life. We mostly talked about high school because we'd just graduated a year and a half before.

Her story was way more interesting than mine, so I tried to just ask questions and listen. "You lived where?" I asked. "I've lived in Colorado my whole life and have never heard of Tinytown… what could possibly happen in a place so small?" I joked. She smiled and launched into the rocking of my world.

"Maybe this will give you an idea of what happens in Tinytown…" she said as her voice trailed off. "I had a good life." We sat and listened to her story as we sped through the snow covered streets of Denver. The night was so still and picturesque – snowdrifts sparkled with the light from our headlights. Her story ebbed and flowed like the snow-covered hills in the distance. She told us about her tight knit community, committed friends, and relationship with her parents.

Nobody's life is perfect, but my brown-eyed beauty's description of life in Tinytown seemed pretty close to Utopia. I could almost picture the people as she described the local grocery store, the summer street dance, and other events you might find in a normal small town. As she talked, we all chimed in and made a wisecrack or two about her version of Mayberry RFD.

## SUCCESS PROOF

Brown eyes killed the laughter and the good feelings with one little sentence when she said: "And then Angel's accident happened, and everything I knew and believed about Tinytown changed – everything I believed about the universe changed." It was like one of those scenes in a movie when everything moves in slow motion. I was so enthralled with this girl and her story, and she had me hanging on every word.

She continued, "My best friend Angel barely survived a deadly car crash her senior year... the doctors told us it was 'touch and go' as they revived her several times.

"Our only hope was for her to survive, so that's what we prayed for... I haven't really told this to anyone else, but sometimes I wish we would have prayed differently."

The words hung in the air like a thick snow cloud.

After a long pause she continued, "Angel did survive, but she is trapped in a body so badly damaged that she can't talk or walk anymore.

"When we first went to see her in the hospital, she looked so peaceful lying there with her beautiful golden hair splashing on her pillow – she was so beautiful." They waited for Angel to be "normal" again, but life often changes in a moment. Life was never the same for the brown eyed beauty.

She told us how her life imploded. She fought with her parents, and eventually vowed to leave home and never come back. As soon as high school was done, she moved out and started working a dead end job. Tinytown was no longer paradise. Instead, it became a reminder of the cruelty of life. Even though I hadn't known her for long, I was heart broken as she talked about how empty and lonely she felt inside.

"You know, I was really angry at God," she said with an edge in her tone. "Seriously God!?," she said clenching her fists, "Why did you cause something Angel and her family to suffer?" No one dared speak. "So I said to God, 'If you're real, why don't you show yourself to me?'" More silence.

"And He did," she added.

Time out. The rest of the story might make some of you uncomfortable. But I have to say, it is the part of the story that drew me very close to this remarkable woman. This is the best part of the story because it was a big "A Ha!" moment for me. And, it's the best way to conclude my book.

She pushed through her story, "Shortly after I told God off and asked for some proof, He appeared to me in a very vivid way," Brown Eyed Beauty paused and then said, "I saw a vision of Jesus Christ hanging on a cross.

"It was horrifying to see that His beard had been plucked out of his face and his hair was matted with blood."

I didn't know if I was supposed to be happy or sad in the moment. I do know I had goose bumps and a lump in my throat. She didn't wait for us to take a breath when she asked, "Do you want to know what He said?"

Three other heads in the front row of the brown land barge bobbed in unison.

"We were eye to eye and He said, 'Mary, while I was on this cross, I was thinking about you.'"

# SUCCESS PROOF

A couple of miles passed by while we thought about the implications of her statement. She admitted that she was still working through Angel's condition, but I got the sense she wasn't wondering "why" God allowed the accident to happen. The God sized statement is this, "Let me worry about Angel… I want you to get a glimpse of the most important, real and game changing thought you will ever have… I love you beyond your very small view of the universe… and that's enough."

The scene of that night races through my mind often. Her vision changed my life. I learned two things: bad things are going to happen in this world, AND God is still preeminent. Even if the whole worlds seems like it's falling apart, I am convinced that God is good. For the record, God has to be the one to convince you of that truth. Just ask Him to "show Himself to you"… He just might.

From that night forward, I was convinced I needed to marry the brown eyed beauty. I could see her connection to God was deep… it was real… and I wanted nothing less for my own life.

In a word, Jesus was clearly preeminent in her life.

And yes, she did eventually say, "Yes!" to my proposal. The glue holding us together is an unwavering belief in a real God who can carry us through hard times – and even good ones. You see, the good moments are probably more difficult to handle in ministry than the bad ones. Good times often serve as a very subtle trap. Most pastors don't even realize they are drifting.

JASON HANSELMAN

The constant battle is to keep Jesus preeminent.

[pree-**em**-*uh*-n*uh* nt] adjective

1. eminent above or before others; superior; surpassing: *He is preeminent in his profession.*

## Who is Really Preeminent?

When you meet God, your world suddenly shrinks and enlarges all at the same time. You would think pastors would understand this concept well. We don't. Even pastors with churches of 20, 50 or 200 believe they are on a more noble pastoral pursuit than the rock star pastor types. Small numbers and dwindling churches defend their numbers in such spiritual tones. They say, "Famous pastors are only interested in 'tickling the ears' of this generation; or, only the 'narrow road' and 'small gate' leads to heaven." Really? I think a lot of those kinds of pastors are the other side of the rock star coin.

Think about it. Some small church guys are mini-me rock stars. They do their best to gather a bunch of groupies to heap accolades on them. The sheep show up every week to tell their pastor how much they admire his teaching, his family, and his stance for Biblical purity. Eventually, a pastor will do whatever it takes to protect his reputation and ministry with his group of people. Others think they have to defend God's reputation (that's a whole different book)! Or, they have to be ready to tell those people what to think about political and social issues. "Normal" people couldn't possibly discern those things on their own. The bottom line is this: rock stars crave the center of attention. You don't need a huge ministry to look like a rock star.

# SUCCESS PROOF

Even as I was writing this book, I stumbled on a Facebook post blasting the work of a world famous Christian leader. The leader has a new book coming out, and someone (other than the leader) is promoting the book on his wall. The post had hundreds of comments. Naturally, I was curious to read the comments. The majority of the comments criticized the leader for one thing: his ministry is growing.

So, I did a little investigation and clicked on the names of the people who were especially critical in their remarks. It was no surprise to find that many of the most toxic comments came from... drum roll please... church leaders. How do I know they are leaders? Their profile lists their occupation and workplace. Many of them were engaged in the same kind of self-promotion for their own churches and sermons! The difference must be in the size of the audience these mini-me rock stars attract.

Social media is the new bully pulpit in America.

What do we expect? Churches hire twenty-something's to stand on a stage under bright lights in front of an audience and communicate deep spiritual things. Mix in the fact that most of the people in the ministry business are outgoing and have a need to be liked. When you mix a person with a need to be liked with an opportunity to perform on stage, you get a volatile reaction. Even the most humble pastor can get caught up the rock star mentality -- especially when someone decides to make a major life change as a result of the sermon he preaches.

I'm guilty. I know there were many times when I would show up at a church service or in a board meeting thinking I was the best or smartest person in the room. Even if Jesus

Christ walked in, I would probably thank Him for attending and then launch into my little talk. After all, He would probably enjoy my humor and handling of the Biblical text.

I don't know how other pastors handle "success." Most of the good times in my life were quickly followed by moments of disaster. I don't like pain, but it has always forced me to remember what I learned more than 20 years ago in the front seat of the brown land barge – Jesus is still thinking about me, and He's still good. Either I'm Pollyannaish (and believe fairy tales) or God is cruel (because He wants to ruin my prosperity). Neither is true. My hope isn't determined by my circumstances, and when I examine the history of my life I can see God has been far more kind than evil to me.

## Avoiding Extremes

The point of this chapter is to simply explore how "normal" hard working pastors can avoid one of two extremes. I am very comfortable with the fact that I was never destined to be "the guy" or a rock star at a Cool Church. Some guys never come to grips with this reality. Almost every time I get together with other pastors for a "prayer" meeting the focus is on church size, leadership, or the latest buzz in ministry. I understand we need to talk shop, but it's deeper than that. I think it's a ploy to make ourselves look more important than we really are. The guys with the coolest and best churches were envied, and the rest of us either got bitter or made a play to get hired at their church.

There's nothing wrong with wanting to work for a church with more opportunities. I simply want a place where I can

## SUCCESS PROOF

live out my giftedness, love God, and serve others. So many pastors are looking for the same thing, but we're having trouble cutting through the clutter to find a ministry where Jesus is preeminent. How do I know? The 1000 Honeymoon Cycle is alive and well in American churches. When we buy into a ministry where the Rock Star Pastor is only living to make his dreams come true, a lot of us non-rock star types get wounded in the fall out.

As I was writing this chapter, God reminded me again of His preeminence through my new friend, and supervisor at work, Giant Joe. At six foot four, and more than 200 pounds, Joe's physical presence is intimidating at first. Giant Joe is an ex-marine and knows how to hold a "command presence" in front of a group. The tough guy persona melts away the moment you meet him. Giant Joe is all smiles and handshakes. Few people are as easygoing and affable.

We hit it off from day one, mainly I think because Giant Joe is a recovering pastor like me (he's recovering from a long stint in ministry too). If anyone has reason to steep in bitterness, it's Giant Joe.

He shared his story about a conflict in his ministry with his old boss. Essentially, Joe worked with a senior pastor who grew jealous of Giant Joe's popularity with the people of the church. "He started to make unreasonable demands and have me out calling on people every night of the week," Giant Joe lamented. "No way was I going to do that when my kids were so young."

Eventually, Giant Joe quit on ministry and left church work to assemble widgets in a factory.

"Jason, I didn't learn what was really going on behind the scenes at the church until I bumped into the youth minister several years after I resigned," added Giant Joe. "I was surprised when the youth minister asked if he could apologize… but I had problems with the senior pastor and not him." To Giant Joe's shock, the youth pastor told Giant Joe that the senior pastor was secretly slandering the Giant's reputation with other staff members and board leaders.

"I was stunned. In fact, I was even angry with God," he said with an edge to his tone. Learning about the senior pastor's deception didn't make him feel justified about leaving ministry especially considering his family suffered needlessly when he lost work. He looked me right in the eye and said, "And then my worst nightmare came true when I broke down and decided to ask my parents for a loan… it was only for five hundred bucks, but I didn't see any other way to pay the bills and put food on the table."

God saw another way. An unsolicited and anonymous person sent a check for five hundred dollars– the very day they were going to ask for a loan. I'm not saying God is going to send everyone a $500 check in the mail, but I am saying He will not let your suffering be in vain. Thankfully, God rescued Giant Joe in time. Otherwise, he might have given up too soon. Now, Giant Joe is the department head of a growing ministry in the Midwest.

Yes, God came through in a big way for Giant Joe, but the moral of the story is not this: God will make all your hopes and dreams come true if you pray hard enough. Sorry, but you can't "faith" God into anything. Ever. Instead, the real encouraging news is this: ministry is hard, and God is good.

# SUCCESS PROOF

I need to compare the Giant's story with Plato the Philosopher. My first encounter with Plato was at No Name U. I was standing outside the front door at No Name when the Philosopher rode up on his mountain bike. He made a grand entrance by hurdling over his handlebars and executing a beautiful face plant on the sidewalk. We officially met him after his brief stay in the ER… and six stitches in his face.

The Philosopher wanted to evangelize people in the farthest corner of the world after he finished his studies at No Name U. And he did. He got a degree and a wife (I think a wife came with every degree at the school) and they went to some tribal country in Africa. Raising enough funding, securing government paperwork and enduring the necessary inoculations is no small feat, but they did it in record time. All signs pointed to long term success for the Philosopher.

We loved reading his email updates about witch doctors, African culture and their struggle to survive in the bush. Plato was not into the "typical" missionary activities (like building church buildings and singing American hymns in them). His favorite concept was "Business as Mission." I won't go into all the details of BAM, but the philosophy is an out of the box method for sharing the Gospel.

And then, life changed in a moment. The Philosopher's youngest child developed a virus and the local hospital botched a procedure. In fact, the situation was so serious that I flew with a buddy to Africa to offer support. We agonized and prayed for God to be merciful. The child survived, but only to suffer major medical complications. In a matter of months, the Philosopher and his family came back to America because their child requires substantial medical care.

Losing a job is one thing, but the potential of losing a child is a completely different level. The Philosopher and his wife did not pretend everything was "fine." How could they? Their child will never be what the world calls "normal" again. Imagine deciding to sell all of your possessions, live on the meager donations of others, and suffer through intense culture shock only to have your dream shattered by the malpractice of a medical doctor in a foreign country.

The Philosopher and I have had some intense conversations about his story. He is not bitter and he has not given up on God. He was convinced about the preeminence of God before the tragedy struck ... and I think it has made all the difference. Plato has an unbelievable trust in God, and from what I can see, most of it stems from his life without Christ. Over and over he talks about the despair and shame he experienced before someone introduced him to Christ. And now, even though his life got a lot more painful, he knows God is present and will provide enough mercy and grace for him to endure.

## Megaphones

All three of the people in this chapter are good examples of the kinds of people I have known in ministry over the past two decades. Their raw stories are sources of encouragement to me to keep on looking for a better way to live out my life in ministry. Not all stories have happy endings in ministry. I know of others who have decided to simply throw in the towel and leave the pain of church work. My heart breaks for them.

## SUCCESS PROOF

My pain and struggle are not unique. The challenge, as I'm learning now, is to make Jesus preeminent. Either he owns the stage or I do. He handles the role of Rock Star way better than I do anyway.

In many respects, the conclusion of this book is just the beginning of a whole new chapter in my life. For once, I think I've found my calling… and the struggle to get to where I am at now was worth it. Maybe you will find the same thing. CS Lewis describes it best, "Pain insists upon being attended to. God whispers to us in our pleasures, speaks in our consciences, but shouts in our pains. It is his megaphone to rouse a deaf world." Listen. Learn. Grow into who God wants you to be. Nothing more. Nothing less.

# Study Guide provided by Gerry Erffmeyer

Gerry Erffmeyer has been a pastor in 4 different churches spanning 44 years in the Christian Reformed Church. He is presently the chaplain at Park Place of Elmhurst in Elmhurst Illinois. He has a passion for reaching out to help other pastors who are struggling with circumstances in their ministries.

## Chapter 1: The Leadership Obsession

--Has anyone ever asked you the Question on Page 14: "Do you believe you were made for something great?" How would you answer?

--Comment on the statement on Page 15: "I was like a lot of other pastors I know. We blame our lack of greatness on other people and circumstances…"

--Page 17 – Do you feel like Jason: "I'm disappointed in the way so many church leaders worship leadership."

--Page 21: "The mark of greatness is not how many people are following your idea, it's how you steward the responsibilities God has given you." Do you agree?

## Chapter 2: Greatness at the Expense of People

--Page 28: "The truth is, I was in love with the idea of success." - Has that been true about you?

## Chapter 3 The End of a Dream: Betrayal in Ministry

--Page 33 "I was learning that "real" leaders never admit fault. It is the job of the leader to assign blame…" Have you ever been in a situation in a church where you experienced this?

--"My confidence as a leader vanished. I was angry with myself…In a lot of ways I blamed myself…" Has that ever happened to you?

--Page 36: "One of the greatest gifts in the world is to discover the one thing that drives you, or the thing that you believe is your main purpose in life." How would you describe the one thing that drives you?

--Page 39: "You still need to be comfortable with finding and living out your purpose, even if it means something that never gets "noticed." Do you agree?

--Page 40: "I needed to let some of my dreams die." Has that happened to you?

## Chapter 4 "Boredom is the Real Cause of Burnout in Ministry"

--Page 43: Pastors are adrenaline junkies..." Do you agree?
--Page 44: "The only problem is the Monday morning crash" Have you experienced that?
--Page 48: "I'm guilty of holding churches in contempt because they did not share my vision, which was really a vision about building my own empire."   Is that true of you?

## Chapter 5 "Church HR Is Not Working and Why No One Wants To Fix It"

--Page 54 "The hiring process in churches is an abysmal failure." Do you agree?
--Page 55: "The results of pandering to tradition, leveraging power and cultivating pride are obvious: ruined lives and anemic churches." "The result is 1500 pastors leaving the ministry every month"   Do you agree that these are major problems in churches today?

## Chapter 6: "Food Stamps, Counselors and Airports: Sometimes you need to Hit Rock Bottom"

--Have you ever felt that you've hit rock bottom because of pain you've experienced in trying to lead churches?
--Comment on page 71: "Seeking help from a mental health professional is not a sign of weakness or a denial of God's power."
--Page 80 – Are you surprised by Jason's statement: "Working at the airport helped me re-establish my love for people."

## Chapter 7 "Be Who You Are. Nothing More. Nothing Less."

--Page 83 - "For youth pastors, the Holy Grail was to have fun, get kids excited about their faith, and maybe find God somewhere in the middle of it." Have you found this to be true?

--Page 93 – Numbers 13:33 We even saw giants in the land there...next to them we felt like grasshoppers and that's what they thought, too." When you look at the rock star pastors, you're nothing but a grasshopper, and your contributions in this world are nothing compared to them." Do you agree?

--What do you think of Jason's advice – Page 94: "Be who you are. Nothing more, nothing less."

## Chapter 8: "Mentors Matter"

--Page 98 "He helped me plant a church and it worked back then because he kept our focus on other people rather than ourselves." Have you also found this to be true?

## Chapter 9 "Bored Meetings, Mad Bosses and New Beginnings"

--Page 108  Do you agree with Jason's statement: "Few pastors in small churches are ever given the freedom to make decisions"?

--Page 109: "The church was going to lay off staff to "solve the money problem" "The highest value for many of the people attending the church was to see money in the bank.". Have you ever served a church like that?

--Page 120: "In spite of my bad choices, angry disposition and raging depression, God was doing something amazing." Page 121: "My attitude was to be angry at God and almost throw in the towel." Have these sentences ever described what you were going through?

## Chapter 10: The Impact of Small Churches

--Page 132: "The Lone Ranger church prevented a lot of kids from straying from their faith because of a few very committed volunteers who were active in the lives of their youth. Children were loved and accepted." Do you see special benefits in a small church with one Pastor?

## Chapter 11 "Better than a Rock Star"

--Discuss this statement on Page 139: "The good moments are probably more difficult to handle in ministry than the bad ones. Good times often serve as a very subtle trap. Most pastors don't even realize they are drifting. The constant battle is to keep Jesus preeminent."

--Page 140: Eventually a pastor will do whatever it takes to protect his reputation and ministry with his group of people." Is that true?

--Page 141: "Social media is the new bully pulpit in America" Do you agree?

Page 147: Jason's conclusion is from CS Lewis: "Pain insists upon being attended to. God whispers to us in our pleasures, speaks in our consciences, but shouts in our pains. It is his megaphone to rouse a deaf world." Listen Learn. Grow into who God wants you to be. Nothing more. Nothing less. Does this help you as you sometimes struggle with what is happening in your ministry?

www.ingramcontent.com/pod-product-compliance
Lightning Source LLC
LaVergne TN
LVHW090116080426
835507LV00040B/915